SpringerBriefs in Law

More information about this series at http://www.springer.com/series/10164

Charles Foster · Jonathan Herring

Altruism, Welfare and the Law

Springer

Charles Foster
Green Templeton College
University of Oxford
Oxford
UK

Jonathan Herring
Exeter College
University of Oxford
Oxford
UK

ISSN 2192-855X ISSN 2192-8568 (electronic)
SpringerBriefs in Law
ISBN 978-3-319-21604-1 ISBN 978-3-319-21605-8 (eBook)
DOI 10.1007/978-3-319-21605-8

Library of Congress Control Number: 2015944508

Springer Cham Heidelberg New York Dordrecht London

Printed on acid-free paper

Springer International Publishing AG Switzerland is part of Springer Science+Business Media (www.springer.com)

Foreword

Given the centrality to family law of the concepts of welfare and best interests, it is noteworthy, though probably unsurprising, that judges have tended to show little curiosity in teasing out what these very familiar words mean. More puzzling is why the Academy should have shown so little interest.

There is an important doctoral thesis waiting to be written on the history of the welfare principle and of how the understanding and application of the concept has changed down the years. It would require the skills of someone who is both a black-letter legal historian and a legal sociologist, which is perhaps why it has not yet been done.

This is not that book, but it is, if anything, even more important. It is an examination of the issue from an ethical and philosophical perspective by two distinguished academics. They emphasise the importance of understanding the particular unique child or incapacitous adult in the particular circumstances he or she is in *and the relationships within which the child or incapacitous adult lives.* They argue that our task is to enable children and adults lacking capacity to flourish *in the context of good relationships.* But, they emphasise, *good relationships entail give and take, and responsibilities as well as rights.* Accordingly, they suggest, properly understood, the notions of well-being and best interests include relationality, altruism and virtue.

At first blush, this may seem strange to the lawyer accustomed to the dogma that the court is concerned with the interests of parents and third parties only in so far as they bear on the welfare of the child or incapacitous adult; as our authors put it, the routine assumption that the only relevant perspective is that of the child or incapacitous adult, viewed as an atomistic entity. The authors provocatively argue, however, that their analysis is consonant with the way the courts have in fact understood welfare and best interests, that their explanation of best interests and welfare merely makes explicit what the courts *are* actually doing. This is heady stuff, which they seek to make good by an interesting analysis of a number of recent cases. Finally, they test their arguments, and the principles they claim to have derived from them, against six problems of real life.

The thesis is clearly and attractively presented and compellingly argued. It carries conviction. It even provides, it might be thought, the answer to a long-standing problem for which the courts have never had a coherent solution. How is the judge to give effect to the welfare test when faced with two children whose interests conflict? Even more puzzling, how is the judge to decide between the conflicting interests of a child and her mother when the mother is herself a child?

Readers—and I hope that many family lawyers and family judges will read this book—must decide for themselves whether or not they are persuaded. What is apparent, however, is that our authors have given us all—dare I say, judges in particular—much to think about.

May 2015 James Munby

Contents

Chapter 1
Introduction

Abstract This chapter introduces the themes we explore in the book. When a person is unable to make a decision for herself others need to make the decision on her behalf. This is typically done based on an assessment of what is in that person's best interests, or what will best promote her welfare. This, we argue, entails an understanding of the Good Life. We argue that the Good Life, properly understood, does not consist in the selfish pursuit of one's own happiness, but is characterised by altruism, virtue and good relationships.

Keywords Best interests · Welfare · Well-being · Capacity · Virtue · Altruism

Facts matter. However learned a judge may be, unless she makes the right findings of fact, her judgment is unlikely to be right.

Similarly, unless the substantive law makes correct factual assumptions about its subjects, it is unlikely to be satisfactory.

The subjects of the substantive law are human beings. The idea of law is intrinsically offensive: laws compel us to do things, or not to do things, or to do or not do things in particular ways. Any law takes a good deal of justifying. The justification can only be that it improves the lives of its subjects: in short, that it tends to maximise human flourishing.

Implicit in every law, therefore, is the assumption that it maximises human flourishing. And implicit in that assumption (but rarely discussed), is a view of what human beings are—and hence what is good for them. Anthropology precedes jurisprudence. Or it should.

Our contention in this book is that the dominant anthropology of law-makers (both legislators and judges) is wrong. Law-makers have adopted uncritically the pastiche of human nature which dominates the thinking of unnuanced free-market capitalism. Humans, according to this account, are selfish atomistic entities: like billiard balls wearing City suits. Such humans have no difficulty identifying themselves. 'I am John Smith', one of them will say, and will wholly fail to understand that many questions are begged by that formulation. Nor will they have any difficulty identifying their desires: 'I want to accumulate wealth, and die before getting Alzheimer's disease'. When they talk about who they are and what they

C. Foster and J. Herring, *Altruism, Welfare and the Law*,
SpringerBriefs in Law, DOI 10.1007/978-3-319-21605-3_1

want, there will be no mention of any other people. They owe nothing to anybody. They came from nowhere, are entirely self-made and have no dependents. No one will weep when they die, and nor should they.

We have not met anyone like this. This is not just because we live a cloistered life in Oxford, and ought to get out more. People like this simply don't exist. Accordingly a law based on their needs will be misconceived. Furthermore, if people like that did exist, the law should try to stop them from behaving in the ways that they do behave. It should try to stop them both in their own interests and in the interests of the other people in the society of which they are a part.

As a matter of basic biology, geography and sociology the atomistic claim is ludicrous. We share 99.8 % of our DNA with chimpanzees, and rather more with other humans. Everyone is at least a cousin. We did not contribute anything at all to our own genetic burden, to our own arrival in the world, or to the first few years in it. Even if we live in the most tightly hermetically sealed environment, exercising obsessive control over everything possible, we will not escape disease or death. Hermetically sealed environments would not be good for humans, as we will discuss, and in practice they don't exist. Fate, love, bosses, slips, trips, and the infuriating, exhilarating, painful, polishing, ecstatic, irritating slide of one human's skin against that of another are our lot. We have to live with it, and the law should too.

Why has the law failed so abjectly?

There are many reasons.

One is that that lawmakers themselves tend to see themselves as exemplars of the self-determining pastiche. And so they shape laws which embody as an ideal their narcissistic self-portrait.

Another is that the pastiche at least has the virtue of simplicity. It is far, far harder to legislate for the messy reality. It might be argued that it is impossible. We will deal with that objection in due course. We do acknowledge that simplicity is desirable in the law, and that workability is essential. But where the simple solution is plainly wrong, we hesitate to endorse it. The law can do better. It has shown that it can.

Yet another reason is that much of the law is concerned with situations where the pastiche produces workmanlike solutions. The law of contract is the obvious example. Contract is concerned with situations where X knows exactly what he wants from Y, Y has agreed that X should have it, and yet Y has defaulted. It is correct in these circumstances that the law should enforce the agreement. But this model has metastasized out of the commercial court into other areas of the law. It has sometimes done great harm. Many of our most influential jurists have cut their teeth on and paid their mortgages by the law of contract, and when they come to give judgments in areas other than contract, they tend to bring to those areas contract's rather simple and sclerosed assumptions about the needs and nature of the litigants.

There are two areas of the law where these assumptions most obviously fail to do the job: family law relating to children, and those parts of medical law that relate to decisions made on behalf of patients lacking capacity. In both these cases English law demands a consideration of the welfare or the best interests of the child/patient.

The concepts of welfare and best interests play a central role in medical and family law.

Section 1 of the Children Act 1989 provides:

When a court determines any question with respect to

(a) the upbringing of a child; or
(b) the administration of a child's property or the application of any income arising from it, the child's welfare shall be the court's paramount consideration.[1]

In the case of adults lacking capacity, s 1(5) of the Mental Capacity Act 2005 provides: 'An act done, or decision made, under this Act for or on behalf of a person who lacks capacity must be done, or made, in his best interests.'

The welfare principle in the Children Act and the best interests test in the Mental Capacity Act 2005 have generated plenty of academic and judicial discussion (Herring 1999a, b, 2014a; Eekelaar 2002; Donnelly 2010; Coggon 2010). There is, of course, fierce debate about what, on the facts of a particular case, the tests require—for instance whether a contact order is beneficial to a child, or whether it is in the best interests of a person lacking capacity to be involved in research. But, the debate often tacitly assumes that all the parties agree about the definition of the terms 'welfare' or 'best interests', and that there is therefore no need to question those definitions. In particular, it is routinely assumed that the only relevant perspective is that of the child or incapacitous adult, viewed as an atomistic entity.

Medical and family lawyers (e.g. Eekelaar 2002; Herring 2008) have been troubled by cases where there are two possible decisions:

(a) a decision which benefits slightly the individual in question, but causes major harm to the family or carers, and
(b) a decision which harms the individual slightly, but is a huge benefit to the family or carers.

At first sight the welfare principle or best interests test would appear to mandate (a) and outlaw (b). In *Re P (Contact) (Supervision)* (1996, p. 328) it was held that when considering the welfare principle 'the court is concerned with the interests of the mother and the father only in so far as they bear on the welfare of the child'. Similarly the best interests test under the Mental Capacity Act 2005, Section 4(7) appears to allow consideration of the views of carers *only* in so far as they relate to the best interests of the individual. It may seem, then, that the courts are expected to make best interests determinations by looking solely at the interests of the child or incapacitous adult, ignoring the impact of the decision on anyone else.

[1] Adoption and Children Act 2002, s 1 similarly provides that when a court or adoption agency is coming to a decision relating to the adoption of a child, '[T]he paramount consideration … must be the child's welfare, throughout his life,' s 1(2). This changed the previous position under the Adoption Act 1976, s 6, by which the child's welfare was the first, but not the paramount, consideration.

But life is not so simple. Nor should the law be. We argue here that the court should not use (and in some instances has not used) the welfare or best interests test in such a narrow way. The interests of parents, friends, family members and carers should be and have been taken into account. However, this has often not been done explicitly. We argue that the courts should have no qualms about being explicit.

In this book we explore some of the philosophical, historical and scientific material on well-being. In doing so we hope to reveal some issues that are rarely considered expressly by the courts. We argue that a proper understanding of a person's well-being can require decisions to be made which will primarily benefit (or appear primarily to benefit) another person. We argue that the well-being of a person cannot be assessed in isolation, and that it is only by considering the network of relationships within which a person lives that well-being can be properly considered. Finally, we will argue that meeting one's obligations and cultivating virtues are both aspects of well-being. We thus challenge the assumption that deciding what is in a person's welfare or best interests involves considering solely matters relating to them or the impact of the decision on them. In other words, a judge properly applying the welfare principle or the best interests test should decline to make an order which causes significant harm to others in order to procure a small gain for the child or incapacitous adult.

Suppose, for instance, that a patient is in a minimally conscious state. The family and carers make a (resisted) application for a declaration that it is in the patient's best interests for life-sustaining treatment to be withdrawn. Using our model, it might be argued that the failure to grant the declaration caused significant harm to the patient's relatives and loved ones, while giving little benefit to the patient. If that is right, then, *since the patient's own welfare, broadly viewed, should be assumed to encompass a wish to deny detriment to his relatives/loved ones*, it may be right to grant the declaration. But is this the right way to view welfare/best interests?

We contend that behind judicial determinations of 'welfare', at least in England and Wales, there lies an essentially Aristotelian notion of the 'good life', and that an essential component of the 'good life' is that humans are quintessentially relational beings. One of the ways in which this relationality is expressed is by the courts' recognition that there will be circumstances in which it is in the child's/the incapacitous adult's best interests/welfare to act towards a third party in a way which, viewed objectively, seems altruistic. That approach, we suggest, is correct. It is concordant with the known facts about human beings. It is to those facts, and the philosophical work woven around them, that we now turn.

References

Coggon J (2010) Doing what's best: organ donation and intensive care. In: Danbury C et al (eds) Ethics and law in critical care. Oxford University Press, Oxford

Donnelly M (2010) Determining best interests under the Mental Capacity Act 2005. Med Law Rev 19:27–43

Eekelaar J (2002) Beyond the welfare principle. Child Family Law Q 14:237–256
Herring J (1999a) The Human Rights Act and the welfare principle in family law: conflicting or complementary? Child Family Law Q 11:223–243
Herring J (1999b) The welfare principle and the rights of parents. In: Bainham A, Lindley B, Richards M (eds) What is a Parent?. Hart, Oxford
Herring J (2008) Caregivers in medical law and ethics. J Contemp Health Law Policy 25:1–24
Herring J (2014) Medical Law and Ethics, 5th edn. Oxford University Press, Oxford

Chapter 2
Altruism and Community: A Biological and Philosophical History

Abstract This chapter outlines the biological, cultural and philosophical history of altruism and virtue. It seeks to demonstrate that altruism and virtue are important constituents of our evolutionary inheritance, and that communities and individuals who ignore them are acting against the constitution of human beings, and are hence unlikely to flourish.

Keywords Selfishness · Virtue · Altruism · Community · Religion

2.1 Introduction

'Selfishness is desirable'. No one, anywhere or at any time, has seriously argued this. The proposition seems plainly ridiculous. Yet many systems—of which dog-eat-dog, laissez-faire capitalism is the obvious example (and, yes, the plainest straw man)—have built teetering superstructures on this (always unstated) premise. Hobbes, the world-weary High Priest of egotism, came the closest to deprecating altruism. But still he was not very close. He simply saw altruism as impossible. Apparent altruism was always more or less well-disguised egoism. 'We're all irredeemably selfish', he held, despairingly, and the Darwinists cheered. But things have moved on in biology since then, and back in philosophy.

We are not concerned in this book with the reasons for the yawning disparity between what people acknowledge is good behavior and the behavior that, by their actions, they endorse. We merely note, first, that, whenever serious people have sat down and reflected, they have concluded that altruism and community are good things and that selfishness is not a good thing; and, second, that altruism and community are workable: there is a practical alternative to social Darwinism hasn't been reluctantly agreed because there is no alternative. Co-operative, mutually supportive societies exist and thrive. There are many, many altruistic individuals: they are feted by their communities, and, as we will see, have many significant advantages over their self-centred peers.

C. Foster and J. Herring, *Altruism, Welfare and the Law*,
SpringerBriefs in Law, DOI 10.1007/978-3-319-21605-3_2

This chapter reviews the biological and sociological facts that pertain to altruism and community. It then moves on to consider the way that altruism and community have been viewed by the some of the great thinkers.

Valuing community is not, of course, the same as valuing altruism. There is, as we will see, an etymological connection between altruism and community, but this does not denote any necessary substantive connection between the two. One could have a model of social cohesion that expressly acknowledged necessary interdependence, and yet perpetuated selfish exploitation. Again, we do not explore that possibility, but simply observe that such a society would not be endorsed either by our deepest intuitions or by the people to whom we credit the best thinking.

2.2 The Evolution of Altruism and Community

One cannot coherently start anthropology by looking just at *anthropos. Homo sapiens* is a very recent arrival on the planet, and she gets all her physical building bricks from stardust, via amoeba, worms, and shrews, and most of her psychology from the Upper Palaeolithic, via lemurs.

For a long time life was a soup of individual, one-celled organisms. But natural selection decreed that co-habitation was the way forward. This cohabitation was of two kinds: clumping and inhabitation. Parts of the soup began to coagulate into communities: coral reefs—massive cities of intimately adjacent individuals—are a good and early example. And, early too, one organism came to live inside another. The mitochondria that generate energy inside our own complex cells were originally free-living bacteria that saw that it was not good to be alone, and which had skills that won them a place inside the cell membrane of larger organisms.

Complex cells aggregated: clumps differentiated. Multi-cellular organisms rather than mere conglomerations arrived. And now natural selection could start pumping out variety and complexity with exuberant incontinence.

Community and at least apparent altruism in the non-human world are obvious facts. For our purposes it does not matter at all whether the apparent altruism is really disguised selfishness. The mere fact that altruism and community have been generated by a system that has generated us is enough to suggest strongly that if we want to live in accordance with our own constitution (which is likely to be concordant with, if not necessary to, our thriving) we should learn and live by the lessons of altruism and community.

Very broadly, three explanations of altruism are visible through the Darwinian lens. First: kin selection (Smith 1964; Eberhard 1975; Foster, Wenseleers and Ratnieks 2006). I benefit X, even at the cost of a detriment to me, because he shares sufficient genetic information with me for his survival to be statistically worthwhile for me. Scribbling a calculation on the back of a beer mat, Haldane (1926, p. 424) declared: 'I would lay down my life for two brothers or eight cousins.' The figures are neat: on the face of it they explain the suicidal heroism of social insects who die for the hive: they are all related, of course, to the Queen, and to each other. But in higher animals, and particularly in man, the explanation begins to flounder, mainly because it implies an almost mystical dialogue between an individual and her DNA, whereby the DNA, having presented the individual with the statistical facts, persuades him (often in the course of the split second before he flings himself under the metaphorical bus to save his offspring), that the sacrifice is, on balance, prudent.

Then there is group selection, where altruistic *groups*, rather than individuals, are the subjects of natural selection (Wilson 1975; Wilson and Sober 1994). Altruistic groups may be at an advantage, and of course they will be composed of individuals who themselves display altruism. Orthodox Neo-Darwinism has, in the last few decades, been haughtily dismissive of group selection. There are distinct signs that group selection is being rehabilitated in the biological academy. It makes individual altruism a type of self-interest (altruism is a necessary qualification for membership of a beneficial club), but that is no problem for us.

And finally there is reciprocal altruism, which purports to explain co-operation between non-genetically related individuals (Trivers 1971; Ashton et al. 1998; Wilkinson 1988). It's about back scratching. If you scratch my back I will calculate the net benefit to me and compare it with the net detriment associated with scratching yours. If the benefit outweighs the detriment, I'll scratch: if it doesn't, I won't.

We do not dispute that each of these mechanisms plays some role in producing some of the altruism and community seen in the natural world. Yet we observe the uneasiness with which most professional biologists approach these explanations. Darwin himself was troubled by altruism, feeling (unnecessarily, we think) that if a genuine example of non-human altruism were found, the theory of evolution by natural selection would be in tatters.

However confident biologists are that there is no *real* altruism in the natural world, there is a near consensus that there is *some* real altruism in humans. Some human altruism can no doubt be explained by one of the three mechanisms. Particularly in societies that value altruism (and they are everywhere: but why? we ask) to behave altruistically can increase status, and hence result in some sort of benefit visible to natural selection.

While we are encouraged by this consensus, it is not necessary to our thesis. Even if, properly viewed, all human altruism is in fact disguised selfishness, the disguise is often so thick as to be impenetrable either by the apparent altruist (who cannot consciously perceive the benefit to herself) or by the society that applauds her. Psychologically—and thus ethically—the altruism might just as well be real, whatever Darwin says.

2.3 Religion

Two reasonably safe generalizations can perhaps be made about all the great religions of the world. The first is that the individual believer acknowledges that she herself is not the measure of all things. And the second is that this has some ethical corollaries.

The first of these propositions is expressed in many ways: in creation myths (in none of which is Man generically, or the individual in particular, self-authored); in the identification of the individual believer with a body of believers, or a nation; in redemption narratives (in which, even if the believer has to work out her own salvation, she often still has to get her pass to eternity rubber-stamped by a Divine Judge, who has the last word); and in stories of the Apocalypse, in which a force outside the control of the individual will roll up the world. Even those religions afflicted least by creeds and hierarchies (for instance Buddhism), acknowledge the role played in the fate of an enlightenment-seeking individual by teachers, writings, and the community.

The Judaeo-Christian tradition insists that it was not good for Adam to be alone, and that the company of non-human animals would not suffice. For Adam to thrive he needed 'bone of his bone' to lie beside him, and so woman was created out of his body. We are all the products of that bizarre act of exfoliation and in vitro cell culture. Adam and Eve were commanded to multiply: more is better. The rest of the Hebrew Bible is about how a family became a nation, and about the deeds and misdeeds of that turbulent nation.

Judaism never lost the notion that the vibrant messiness of the family, reflected in the lurching destiny of a nation, was the way to live. To be human, for a Jew, is to be a member of a community—hence Judaism's traditionally liberal attitude towards early abortion: an embryo, according to many commentators, only gets the ful protection of Jewish religious law when it is implanted into the body of the mother—when it is physically grafted into intimate relationship with another human being.

Judaism is about Covenant: about the acknowledgment of mutual responsibility. The demands of the 'I' become subject to the conditions of the covenant, and hence to the interests of the other parties to the covenant. The philosopher of Ecclesiastes is world-weary because he uses so many personal pronouns.

Asceticism never had any place in mainstream Judaism. But it acquired a dishonorable and corrosive place in Christianity.

Paul, despite his impeccable Jewish credentials, was very un-Jewishly cynical about marriage. 'It is better to marry than to burn with passion' (1 Corinthians 7:9), he taught, which is hardly an endorsement, and he urged his followers not to complicate their lives with the burdens of family life: 'I would that you were as I myself am' (1 Corinthians 7:8)—i.e. unmarried. But these comments need to be understood in the context of Paul's apocalyptic expectations. He thought that the time was short, that Jesus was about to return, and that the old order was about to be swept away. There was therefore no point in wasting time on ephemeral distractions such as the family: the priority was evangelism.

Paul was plainly wrong about the apocalyptic timetable. 2000 years later families and community are around, and matter. Yet his mistake set some parts of the Christian church running off down blind alleys from which they have never returned. The two most obvious examples are sacerdotal celibacy and the eremitic tradition. Many thousands of believers have renounced marriage. Some have removed themselves physically from their communities and sat on pillars in the Syrian desert, or in caves on Mount Athos.

We think that these moves were wrong: they were based on the same misunderstanding about divine chronology that Paul had, and we do not think that they maximized the thriving of the individuals who took these routes. Yet the very ways that these celibate ascetics chose to live their lives within the theological strictures indicate just how foundational to human life are community and altruism. Some of the most impressive examples of community are monastic; and the Athonite hermit and the Syrian stylite both insist that they are on the front line of the spiritual battle, tussling with demons for the benefit of the rest of the world.

The second proposition (that there are some ethical corollaries) is uncontroversial. 'The Way of Heaven is to benefit others', taught Lao Tzu. In Buddhism, Avalokita, about to enter Nirvana, looks back and sees a rabbit with a broken leg. Shattered at the sight of the suffering, he vows not to enter Nirvana himself until all other creatures can enter it with him. When Judaism echoes Cain's question 'Am I my brother's keeper?' (Genesis 4:9) it unequivocally answers 'Yes!' Jesus' Good Samaritan expends energy, time and money on another, and is commended (Luke 10:29–37). The characteristics, listed in the Sermon on the Mount, of those who will inherit the Kingdom of Heaven, include being 'merciful', 'poor in spirit', (presumably having a relatively lowly view of oneself), a 'peacemaker', and going two miles out of your way (presumably to help another) when you are asked to go one (Matthew 5–7). 'Do nothing from selfish ambition or conceit', counsels St. Paul, 'but in humility regard others as better than yourselves. Let each of you look not to your own interests, but to the interests of others. Let the same mind be in you that was in Christ Jesus, who, though he was in the form of God, did not regard equality with God as something to be exploited, but emptied himself, taking the form of a slave, being born in human likeness. And being found in human form, he humbled himself and became obedient to the point of death—even death on a cross' (Philippians 2:2–8).

The Hadith of Bukhari relates that a man once asked the Prophet what was the best thing in Islam. The Prophet replied: 'It is to feed the hungry and to give the greeting of peace both to those one knows as to those one does not know.'

2.4 The Classical World

2.4.1 Homer and the Heroic Ideal

Homer's heroes, the spondees of capricious gods and goddesses, were concerned, above all, with their personal honour. Everything is subordinated to the quest for a gilded place in story. Perhaps it is this that makes them flat figures. They are famously unreflective (Jaynes 2000) and, bar the derring do, rather dull. You wouldn't want to sit next to Achilles at dinner, or see your daughter marry

Odysseus. They pride themselves on being superhuman, but in fact, from our perspective, succeed only in being sub-human. They're incomplete, and we locate their incompleteness in their egoism.

Yet even they, the exemplars of icy detachment, do not repudiate community or altruism. While they see conflict as primarily a stage on which they can perform very visible deeds, they have fierce tribal and other loyalties, and sometimes weep when their friends die. Heroic virtue is often seen to consist in altruistic, self-endangering attitudes and acts. A man who abandoned his own camp would be seen as a snake—having abandoned not just the possibility of being named a hero, but also the possibility of being branded a real human being. It is only insofar as they embrace the notions of community and altruism that we now see them as anything but cardboard cut-outs.

2.4.2 From Heroic to Civic Virtues

The subsequent history of classical Greek thinking is the history of a shift of focus away from individual heroes, and towards a concern for the benefit of the *polis*—the civil community, and of increasingly intense reflection on what constitutes human thriving. There is, importantly, a good deal of overlap between these two quests. Very often, as we will see, human thriving is seen as inconceivable without being grafted into a community. Thriving is sometimes seen *as* being so grafted. Or thriving is seen as being, or as including, the possessor of a certain set of virtues—and where this is the case, the list of essential virtues almost always includes the virtue of contributing in some way to the wider community.

The old Homeric heroes were not forgotten, but they were reevaluated critically, and there was an increasing trend towards admiring their communitarian characteristics. This process of reevaluation was complete by the time Virgil looked again at the epic of Troy. A.C. Grayling (2011) observes that while Homer feted Achilles and Odysseus, Virgil was inspired instead by Hector, 'who fought for Troy rather than himself, and had the safety of his wife and family in mind when he went to his fatal confrontation with the grief-enraged Achilles.' Virgil's own hero, Aeneas, is a 'Hector-type hero…who escaped the flames of Troy carrying his father on his back and leading his small son by the hand—a highly significant pair of details—and his escape was the legendary beginning of the adventure of another and indeed greater city, namely, Rome.'

Virgil's path to this extraordinary conclusion—that Rome was built on altruism and community—had been constructed by the Greeks.

Turning his back on the earnest (and prescient) speculations of his predecessors about ontology and natural science, Socrates began a conversation about the nature of the good life that has never stopped. Socrates rarely prescribed. He wouldn't be pressed for an answer, seeing his purpose as the exposure of error, the pricking of bubbles, the encouragement of inquiry, and the establishment of sufficiently definite meanings of the core elements of argument for meaningful discourse to be possible.

He didn't have a philosophy: he simply advocated the process of philosophy. To be a philosopher (in Socrates' own buzzing, anarchic way), was to live the good life. The philosophy was the method; the method was the life.

This is unhelpful, and it does not directly imply anything about altruism or community. For that, we have to look at the way that Socrates did his philosophizing. He didn't do it in a cave on Olympus, alone, or with a group of esoterically inducted initiates. The philosophical life *was* discourse. He led it, loudly, in public spaces in the heart of Athens, and met his death because he was a public philosopher: his teaching was said to have corrupted the youth of Athens. From that we know that the philosophical enterprise—the cornerstone, if not the whole structure, of the Good Life, was inescapably relational in its practice, if not inescapably relational in substance. We can come to a similar conclusion from the writings of his pupil, Plato.

Plato inherited his teacher's conviction that the philosophical life was the good one, but was more prescriptive about what that involved—essentially the sort of personal equilibrium that results from a detailed audit of the claims of all contenders for the truth, and the brokering of a sufficient peace between them. Put like that, it sounds monkish and self-obsessed. And it is true to say that Plato was temperamentally and metaphysically closer to Athos than any of his other colleagues in the golden philosophical age of Athens. But it should not be forgotten that his major work, the *Republic*, is (although Plato tries, unconvincingly, to pass it off as an extended metaphor of the government of the self) a treatise of political philosophy. Its conclusions are often offensive, but that's not the point. The point is that political philosophy—the business of thinking about the relations between humans living together—was thought worthy of extended examination. The existence and intensity of the *Republic,* rather than its contents, signify the perceived centrality of relationality to the entire philosophical project. The *Republic* doesn't assume, like St. Paul, that societies are transient things, unworthy of serious consideration. For Plato, as for all the Greeks, they are here to stay, and it is worth getting them right. If the relations between the constituent elements of the state are not right, the consequences are nasty: conversely, if the balance is right, the state will hum with the same satisfying eudaemonic harmony with which the soul of the right-thinking, right-living philosopher hums. The business of politics is part of the business of ethics, and vice versa.

Socrates passed on the baton to Plato, who passed it to Aristotle. Aristotle had a palpable impatience with metaphysics, and a correspondingly intense focus on the here and now. The association between political concerns and ethical considerations became even tighter and more explicit than it was in the teaching of Socrates and Plato. In the *Nichomachean Ethics* Aristotle felt his way slowly towards an anthropology and a consequent scheme of ethics. For him, the good is what an unsullied nature desires. And what is that? It is *eudaimonia*—sometimes, and inadequately, translated as 'happiness'. It really means 'flourishing', and it connotes a very great deal more than a blithe, smiling face. One will have eudaimonia if one lives life as one should. And how should one live it? In accordance with the way that man naturally is. That is a fecund formulation: we will return to and rely on it when we examine the evidence suggesting that community and altruism are physically and psychologically good for us. For Aristotle, man is naturally a reflective wisdom-seeker. If he seeks wisdom he will be virtuous.

Aristotle lists the virtues as courage, temperance, liberality, magnificence, magnanimity, proper ambition, patience/good temper, truthfulness, wittiness, friendliness, modesty and righteous indignation. All but the first two are not the sort of virtues you need in a solitary cave, and even courage and temperance are best displayed in a social context. All the others are relationship-presuming and/or relationship-building virtues. Seven of the remaining virtues (all those except truthfulness and wittiness) are virtues that, as the Greeks understood them, had an element of altruism. Liberality involves giving things to others. The 'magnificent' man won't be self-glorifyingly magnificent: he will create splendid things of which others will be the beneficiaries. To be magnanimous is a special sort of generosity. Someone who is properly ambitious will be ambitious for the good of the *polis* and the good of his friends. To be patient and display good temper is to hold back oneself and let another have a go. Modesty entails reining in a claim about oneself that might be made. Righteous indignation will often (although not necessarily) be indignation on the part of another.

Friendliness perhaps speaks for itself: a good friend will value people other than himself, and will forgo his own interests in order to serve others better. Yet Aristotle has a very great deal to say about it. Here he is, in *Nichomachean Ethics* 8(1).

> ....a discussion of friendship would naturally follow, since it is a virtue or implies virtue, and is besides most necessary with a view to living. For without friends no one would choose to live, though he had all other goods; even rich men and those in possession of office and of dominating power are thought to need friends most of all; for what is the use of such prosperity without the opportunity of beneficence, which is exercised chiefly and in its most laudable form towards friends? Or how can prosperity be guarded and preserved without friends? The greater it is, the more exposed is it to risk. And in poverty and in other misfortunes men think friends are the only refuge. It helps the young, too, to keep from error; it aids older people by ministering to their needs and supplementing the activities that are failing from weakness; those in the prime of life it stimulates to noble actions-'two going together'-for with friends men are more able both to think and to act. Again, parent seems by nature to feel it for offspring and offspring for parent, not only among men but among birds and among most animals; it is felt mutually by members of the same race, and especially by men, whence we praise lovers of their fellowmen. We may even in our travels how near and dear every man is to every other. Friendship seems too to hold states together, and lawgivers to care more for it than for justice; for unanimity seems to be something like friendship, and this they aim at most of all, and expel faction as their worst enemy; and when men are friends they have no need of justice, while when they are just they need friendship as well, and the truest form of justice is thought to be a friendly quality.
>
> But it is not only necessary but also noble; for we praise those who love their friends, and it is thought to be a fine thing to have many friends; and again we think it is the same people that are good men and are friends (8(1)).

This is a picture of dazzling reciprocity and mutual submission, in which the good of one is found to consist in desiring the good of the other—a formula he makes explicit later in the same passage (8(2) and (3)). He goes on to describe as a degraded sort of friendship the friendship which is based on reciprocal altruism (8(3) and (4)) and to list the benefits of community per se (8(9)).

After Aristotle, philosophers' focus on the common good became much less explicit. This was hardly surprising: the rise of vast empires (notably those of Alexander and Rome) meant that decisions were made in far-distant halls. Earnest discussion in the Areopagus could no longer influence public policy significantly. Philosophers became introspective: they got on with their own lives and enquiries. Aristotle continued to be the main authority on how the inalienable characteristics of *Homo sapiens* should shape public policy if it had a chance to do so, since his ruminations expressly presumed that philosophers could and should shape it.

2.4.3 The Classical World After Aristotle

The Greek world in the Hellenistic and Roman periods was awash with philosophical and religious schools. Of the philosophical schools, three stand out: the Cynics, the Epicureans and the Stoics.

The Cynics were the metaphorically dreadlocked, whistle-playing, dog-on-string-leading anti-establishment radicals of the day. They sought to shake off the shackles of law, tradition and decency, and sought to be self-ruling—subject only to their own desires. It was a hark back, but a crude hark back, to Aristotle. Act in accordance with your essence, Aristotle had taught, and the Cynics took that as a licence for licence. Diogenes, one of the founder of the movement, masturbated openly in public if he felt like it (and always, one suspects, even if he didn't, in order to show himself and others just how free he was). It was all a rather childish reaction to the imperial iron fist, but there is a serious philosophical point in it all—namely that to be natural is to be good: that anthropology implies ethics. They rejected established civil society, but it would be a mistake to think that they rejected relationality itself. Like many modern anarchists, they sought to be themselves in order to be able to enter into free, and hence more meaningful, relationships.

The Epicureans were more interesting. The group met in Epicurus' garden in Athens. And there they talked. The fact of the talking, and the mutual respect it embodied and illustrated, was a big part of the philosophy itself. Friendship (of the expressly altruistic sort extolled by Aristotle) was one of life's deepest pleasures and most significant gifts: the wise philosopher would, because of his wisdom, know both that friendship should be prized, and how to cultivate it. Friendlessness was poverty.

A school so expressly concerned with friendship was unlikely to be uninterested in the *polis,* notwithstanding the limited influence of philosophers, and indeed the Epicureans spoke passionately about the importance of justice, which they saw as based on a social contract entered into by all members of society, and which should create a nexus as tight as the biological strictures linking all the inhabitants of a termite mound.

Epicureanism's quietly ecstatic insistence on simplicity, on the value of companionship, on the centrality to human life of a garden full of friends, has been periodically rediscovered through the ages, with shouts of 'Eureka'. But its main rival, Stoicism, has never been far from the mainstream. Indeed it was often the creed of the mainstream itself. Its insistence on personal responsibility and on looking steadfastly at the worst appealed to kings and emperors—or at least to their PR departments.

Stoicism is based on the very un-Homeric assumption that everyone—not just the anointed favourites of the gods—could possess human dignity. This was a big prize, and was appropriated by acting in a way towards oneself and, crucially, others, that was consistent with that dignity. It imposed duties, and gave status in return. It was deeply and revolutionarily democratic. Those democratic corollaries were acknowledged by some Stoics—and in particular the Roman Stoics such as Seneca—to demand radical changes in the social and political order. What middle class, donnish Greeks talked about, many middle class, politically powerful Romans actively advocated.

With Stoicism, philosophy returned fully to its pre-Platonic metaphysical roots, and, like many of us, it got more metaphysical as it got older. The Stoic Emperor Marcus Aurelius (1946) (Book 7:9 and 13) set it out in his *Meditations*:

> All things are interwoven with one another; a sacred bond unites them; there is scarcely one thing that is isolated from another. Everything is coordinated, everything works together in giving form to the one universe. The world-order is a unity made up of multiplicity: God is one, pervading all things; all being is one.....In a system comprising diverse elements, those which possess reason have the same part to play as the bodily limbs in an organism that is a unity; being similarly constituted for mutual cooperation. This reflection will impress you more forcibly if you constantly tell yourself, 'I am a "limb" (melos) of the whole complex of rational things.' If you think of yourself as a 'part' (meros) only, you have as yet no love from the heart for mankind, and no joy in the performance of acts of kindness for their own sake....

This is an account of the interrelatedness of things and people that sounds frankly oriental to our ears, and which is radically at odds with the hard-carapaced, psychotic individualism model by which (probably through Christianity's interest in the salvation of the *individual* soul), it was long obscured, and often eclipsed, in the West.

2.5 From Antiquity to the Renaissance

We can now speed up and paint with a broader brush, for many of the elements of many of the ideas about community and altruism which subsequently appeared were partial recrudescences or repudiations of many of the ideas we have already met.

Constantine's conversion handed the next millennium of western history to Latin Christianity. With this came, as we have already noted, an interest in personal salvation, but until the Reformation pietists, this did not wholly oust communitarianism. Indeed the Church preached loudly that salvation itself was achieved by being grafted into the Body of the Church; of coming aboard a crowded Ark that alone would float on the floodwaters; of being a citizen of Augustine's City of God.

Augustine's own devotion to communitarianism was diluted by his attraction to Plato's otherworldly metaphysics. Aristotle's stock rose massively in the Christian west when he was championed by Thomas Aquinas, but, although Aquinas referred to Aristotle reverently as 'The Philosopher', Aristotle was, for Aquinas, a tool to be pressed into the service of Catholic apologetics, rather than as the paradigm-smasher he could have been. Aquinas never contradicts Aristotle's view of human thriving, but he baptizes it, and quite a lot of the flavour is washed off at the font. Yet Aquinas was largely responsible for Aristotle lying in wait, ready for the Renaissance.

The war cry of the Renaissance was, of course, the ancient quotation from Protagoras: 'Man is the measure of all things.' It was intended as a direct challenge to the theocratic hegemony. While Protagoras almost certainly meant it to mean something like 'The proper business of philosophy is human happiness' (and that is how it was taken by the Athenians who came after him), the Renaissance humanists took it to say much more: that God should be dethroned as the object of philosophical speculation and artistic and scientific obeisance, and that educated eyes should be turned from the heavens to the earth. Whatever they meant, the new Renaissance humanism brought back into focus the old Greek and Roman interest in the *polis.* Stoicism, often the covert personal faith of Christian rulers, was publicly disinterred and resuscitated. Its belief in the (at least) potential dignity of all humans could not, in the thin totalitarian soil, spring up into real democracy, but the seeds were sown for the Enlightenment: when the revolutionaries eventually took to the streets of Paris proclaiming the Brotherhood of Man, they were being Stoic. But in the meantime, Stoical respect for humans (again, partly as a reaction to monastic disdain for the body, and indeed for the temporal human condition as a whole), flowered into the glorious sprawling human nakedness on the walls of Florentine churches.

The Renaissance was not *expressly* an anti-Christian movement: it could not be. The limit of its express anti-Godness was the shift in focus, and a fully-leaded, de-Aquinased understanding of Aristotle: the here and now mattered, and was to be celebrated. And since part of the here and now was community, that had to be celebrated too, and given more serious philosophical time that it had had. For our purposes, it was the bridgehead between the Stoicism of late antiquity and the tectonic, principled communitarianism of the Enlightenment. The Renaissance tilled the soil from which communitarianism and utilitarianism finally sprang.

2.6 The Enlightenment to the 19th Century

The political philosophy of the Enlightenment (which was the busiest period for political philosophy since the death of Aristotle) was characterized by social contract theories. Hobbes gave birth to the idea of a social contract, but the idea grew to workable maturity under Rousseau and Locke. The details of the various theories do not matter: the significant facts are, first, that society was thought worthy of serious thought at all, and, second, that each member of the society was thought to have a connection, through the contract, with every other member. The Enlightenment, politically, was the age of the recognition of a web. It can be argued whether the idea of the web gave birth to democracy (and eventually the barricades on the streets of Paris), or whether the idea of democracy (founded itself in some convictions about the nature and status of men) generated the idea and ideal of communitarianism. Again, it does not matter. Anthropological facts, of the sort asserted in ancient Athens, were again catalytic in the explosive mix that eventually went up and shattered the entrenched oligarchies of western Europe. All the social contract theorists were, believed, in one way or another, that the way humans were inevitably affected the way that they should be governed. For the dark, pessimistic Hobbes, humans, left to themselves, would generate mutually destructive anarchy: they should therefore be forced to sign the anarchy-quelling social contract, at gun-point if necessary, and their adherence to their contractual obligations should be sternly policed. For Locke and Hume—in many ways old-fashioned natural law theorists, human nature (which included active mutuality and self-effacement), decreed the shape of the natural law under which humans could live best. Rousseau had a similar conviction, but his belief in the importance of relationality was even more explicit: private property (the existence of which was fundamentally inconsistent with that relationality), was therefore inconsistent with the social contract.

The logical consequence of this was utilitarianism—the most extreme philosophical expression of altruism and communitarianism. Its roots are old and controversial, but an important node was, uncontroversially, Jeremy Bentham (1776, preface), whose formulation 'it is the greatest happiness of the greatest number that is the measure of right and wrong' has become the foundational slogan of utilitarianism.

This is too familiar. We tend not to notice what it says about our interconnectedness. Unmitigated (and Bentham himself did not dilute it with any caveats), it is saying that the suffering or death of X is not only justifiable but ethically necessary if it increases the net amount of happiness in the world. Altruism to the point of death is demanded of ethically right-thinking people. The subsequent history of utilitarianism has been the history of insertion of caveats. Most modern utilitarians (e.g. Savulescu 2014) recognize that Bentham's original formulation is too demanding—at least of themselves. The details of that evolution are irrelevant here: the important fact is that utilitarianism became the ruling ethical creed of secular Europe from then on.

It was Bentham's political and legal sensibilities that had spawned this doctrine. Those sensibilities were the most prominent sensibilities of that age. Yet there were many others, and they tended to erode the old-fashioned (and often new-fashioned) but cherished notions of the discrete self. Philosophy of Mind finally struggled free of theology (although many of its architects continued to be deists, or even theists). The cornerstone of the new discipline was Hegel. He thought that we are wholly inaccessible to ourselves as discrete entities. Indeed, he seems often to deny (with the enthusiasm, though not the clarity, of Marcus Aurelius), the very *existence* of the self. How do I know myself, he asked? By looking in the mirror of another, he said. He wrote of 'the self-apprehension of the one in the Other'.[1] Frances Berenson (1982, p. 77) observes that in the opening passage of the Introduction of Hegel's Philosophy of Mind:

> …he recognised a very significant point about self-knowledge - namely that self-knowledge cannot be achieved through mere introspection into my own…. feelings, foibles, habits, likes and dislikes, capacities and so on. I cannot examine the single self and reach any important conclusions because I do not exist in isolation from other selves, and my introspection must of necessity be based on an examination of my relationships with others. Hegel can be taken…to be drawing attention to the importance others play in any serious understanding and knowledge of self…

This was the background as the 19th century dawned. Communitarianism had been expressly explored: it had been hinted that altruism was a corollary. As utilitarianism was developed in the 19th century by Bentham (and, although his commitment to altruism was derailed by his almost psychotic individualism, John Stuart Mill), altruism was increasingly recognized as a player on the philosophical and political stage. Indeed the word altruism was coined then. It was about time that it had a name.

2.7 The 19th Century

Auguste Comte invented both the science of sociology and (probably—it was either him or his teacher, Francois Andrieux) the word 'altruism'. It is derived from the Latin stem word *altrui* (for or to another), and the Greek suffix *-ism*. For Comte, altruism, in the very strong sense in which he understood it, underpinned all ethical behaviour.

For Comte, it was of the essence of altruism that no benefit accrued to the altruist. This extreme view may be etymological in its origin. Comte seems to have coined the word 'altruism' as an antonym of 'egoisme' (egotism). Words acquire lives of their own, and the antonymic parenthood of 'altruism' determined its own exegesis in Comte's lips.

Comte was a thoroughgoing philosophical naturalist, purporting to derive his philosophy from the objective needs of human beings. Society had evolved through theological and metaphysical stages, and had finally arrived at the Positive stage, in which, via the scientific method, it was possible to identify the ways that humans should behave ethically. They should adopt his 'Religion of Humanity', built on altruism, progress and order.[2]

---

[1]Phenomenology, 222.

[2]August Comte, Cours de Philosophie.

Individual and corporate happiness and functionality demanded subordination.

> The individual must subordinate himself to an existence outside himself in order to find in it the source of his stability. And this condition cannot be effectively realized except under the impulse of propensities prompting him to live for others. The being, whether man or animal, who loves nothing outside himself, and really lives for himself alone, is by that very fact condemned to spend his life in a miserable alternation of ignoble torpor and uncontrolled excitement. Evidently the principal feature of progress in all living things is that the general consensus which we have seen to be the essential attribute of vitality should become more perfect. It follows that happiness and worth, as well in individuals as in societies, depend on adequate ascendancy of the sympathetic instincts. Thus the expression, 'live for others,' is the simplest summary of the whole moral code of Positivism (Comte 1973, p. 556).

This, for Comte (1891), mandated radical collectivism, a denial of personal rights, and a disapproval of any sort of self-expression.

> [The] social point of view cannot tolerate the notion of rights, for such notion rests on individualism. We are born under a load of obligations of every kind, to our predecessors, to our successors, to our contemporaries. After our birth these obligations increase or accumulate, for it is some time before we can return any service.... This ["to live for others"], the definitive formula of human morality, gives a direct sanction exclusively to our instincts of benevolence, the common source of happiness and duty. [Man must serve] Humanity, who we are entirely.

It was not surprising that he made enemies. Herbert Spencer (1879), an acolyte of Darwin, saw this sort of subordination as flaccid, effeminate and destructive. No society built on subjection would be smiled on by natural selection, whose agenda was the promotion of the strongest. Whenever altruism existed, it was a by-product of the virile egotism of the naturally selected.

John Stuart Mill was more sympathetic. He (theoretically) applauded altruism, but thought that individuals could not be so comprehensively ignored. They were not ignored by natural selection, and could not be ignored by any sensible political system. Individualism, properly husbanded, should generate altruism, not truncate it (Mill 1906). Looking back over the last 150 years of libertarianism, this belief seems naïve.

The big fact of the 19th century was the explosion into the world, in 1859, of Darwin's '*On the Origin of Species*'. At first blush this appeared, as Spencer said, to indicate that egotism, not altruism, was the basic natural law. It both justified and generated the libertarianism of the age. Yet, as Darwin was better understood, the Spencerian pastiche increasingly floundered. There were communitarian elements in the *Origin*. Darwin had shown that we are all cousins—and this applied not just to members of our own species: we were cousins to all the non-human species too. That made it harder for anyone to boast of his ancestry. It blurred the edges of the individual. As the science of genetics began, the blurring increased. Yes, we are unique, but not terribly unique: much of our DNA is shared.

We have already commented that Darwin was troubled by the existence of altruism. The 'problem' of altruism for orthodox Darwinism has not gone away.

Darwin was seen and is still seen by many as having ushered God out of the world. The 'old' Christian morality, which had been one of the main vessels bearing altruism across the millennia, seemed, for some, and for a while, to have sunk. One might have thought that this would have resulted in altruism itself being discounted—as the final victory of dog-eat-dog social Darwinism. While that may indeed have been the reality of the Victorian factory, it was not what most thinkers advocated. Altruism was still essential. Indeed it was a hallmark of what it meant to be properly human. Strip the redundant, degrading, theological window-dressing from the splendid figure of man, and you could see all the more clearly that he was a creature designed for community and characterized, at his best, by altruistic behaviour. Here, for instance, is George Eliot, a high priestess of 19th century humanism:

> My books have for their main bearing a conclusion without which I could not have cared to write any representation of human life – namely, that the fellowship between man and animals which has been the principle of development, social and moral, is not dependent on conceptions of what is not man: and the idea of God, so far as it has been a high spiritual influence, is the ideal of a goodness entirely human (i.e. an exaltation of the human) (cited Grayling 2011, pp. 170–171).

It seems as if that ancient idea of natural law not only survived Darwin, but prospered because of him.

2.8 The 20th and 21st Centuries

The Russian adventurer, Pietr Kropotkin, bridged not only the 19th and 20th centuries, but also, in many ways, the gulf between 5th century BCE Athens and the philosophical sclerosis of the present day. For Kropotkin, like Aristotle and his forbears, the point of philosophical inquiry was to work out the best way to live, not how best to add footnotes to footnotes. Since we live in this world, that entails knowledge about this world. Hence one should travel, curiously and urgently, collecting information incontinently and seeing how it changed ones view about how to live. That was what Kropotkin did. He had many intellectual passions, but one concerned the question of competition. Was Darwin's prediction right? Was there no true altruism in the natural world? He went to legendarily hostile places to find out—Siberia and Manchuria. Here, if anywhere, where resources were scarce, one would expect to see, starkly, the redness of nature's teeth and claws. But that is not what he saw. Instead he was staggered by the efflorescence of co-operation and altruism. All benefited from this, he concluded (so making an uneasy peace with Darwinism): to give was to get. To be selfish was to be hungry. Altruism was essential to both human and non-human life (Kropotkin 1910). Kropotkin's empirical conclusions were, we will shortly suggest, correct. They have been vindicated by more recent research.

The same insistence on empirical inquiry characterized the work of Pitrim Sorokin, who established the Research Center for Creative Altruism at Harvard in

1949. He aimed to understand the roots of human conflict, and to provide a tool for cutting the roots. Although empiricism was important for Sorokin, he recognized its limits and, attracting the grave suspicion of the academy, drew widely on the mystical traditions of the East, including Christianity (an emphatically Eastern religion before Constantine grafted it into the political Establishment). The great formulations of the mainstream religions were supra-empirical apprehensions of matters that went to the heart of human thriving. These matters were only inaccessible to empiricism because they were so fundamental.

Sorokin (1954)'s anatomy of the roots of conflict was complex and controversial. Its details do not concern us. But the tool does: it was altruism: 'love in action'—'conduct as close as possible to the Sermon on the Mount.' True altruism was performed for no perceived benefit to the performer: people were truly altruistic for no reason that they could specifically identify. The justification lay too deep in psychology or religion or evolutionary biology to be recovered and articulated (Bierwiler 1978). It was motivated by a force that sometimes contended with, and sometimes replaced, other atavistic forces. Yet, once performed, the altruistic act was subjectively perceived to be a benefit of some (usually inchoate) kind to the actor, and its benefits to the wider world were clear and widely rippling. Altruism was a sociological adhesive: it repaired the fractures across communities that generate division, war and individual neurosis.

Durkheim championed a more moderate conception of altruism than Comte's or Sorokin's. For him (by and large, although he was not entirely consistent), altruism did not necessarily imply detriment to the altruist. To the contrary, every individual was necessarily a social creature, and since altruism was essential to the health of that creature, each member of society was the beneficiary of her own altruism. But this did not mean that the individual vanished when properly integrated into her society—as his detailed examination of the question of altruistic suicides demonstrated (Golub 2014, pp. 31–36). Yet morality, for inalienably, quintessentially social animals, was necessarily that which benefited society.

> If each individual taken separately has no moral worth, the sum total of individuals can scarcely have more. The sum of zeros is, and can only be, equal to zero. If a particular interest, whether mine or someone else's, is amoral, several such particular interests must also be amoral. Moral action pursues impersonal objectives. But the impersonal goals of moral action cannot be either those of a person other than the actor, or those of many others. Hence, it follows that they must necessarily involve something other than individuals. They are supra-individual. Outside or beyond individuals there is nothing other than groups formed by the union of individuals, that is to say, societies. Moral goals, then, are those the object of which is society. To act morally is to act in terms of the collective interest. This conclusion imposes itself in the wake of the foregoing arguments, which were successively eliminated. Now, it is evident that a moral act must serve some living and sentient being and even more specifically a being endowed with consciousness. Moral relations are relations between consciousnesses. Above and beyond me as a conscious being, above and beyond those sentient beings who are other individual beings, there is nothing else save that sentient being that is society…. To understand the significance of this major proposition, one must take account of the meaning of society. If we accept what has for a long time been the classical and widely held view, that society is only a collection of individuals, we are thrown back into the foregoing difficulties without any way of surmounting them.

> If self-interest has no moral value for me, it has no more among my fellows whatever their number, and, consequently, the collective interest, if it is only the sum of self-interests, is itself amoral. If society is to be considered as the normal goal of moral conduct, then it must be possible to see in it something other than a sum of individuals; it must constitute a being sui generis, which has its own special character distinct from that of its members and its own individuality different from that of its constituent individuals. In a word, there must exist, in the full meaning of the word, a social being. On this condition only is society able to perform the moral function that the individual cannot (Durkheim 1973).

It was on this Durkheimian foundation that feminist philosophers erected, as a direct challenge to the phallic, macho-atomist model of self-determination that still holds much of (particularly medical) ethics in thrall, the idea of 'relational autonomy.' This insists that our lives are quintessentially interdependent, and that ethical questions about what should be done for X have to be viewed through the lens of X's relationships. A decision about X's medical treatment (for instance), affects not just X, but many others too. For most patients, according to this model, the right question is not 'What is best for me?', but 'Given the responsibilities that I owe to those in relationships with me and the responsibilities owed to me by others, what is the most appropriate course of action?' (West 1997).

We are sympathetic to many of the ambitions and much of the language of relational autonomy. But it suffers from some of the habitual drawbacks of protest movements: a narrowness of vision that comes from having its agenda dictated by that against which it is reacting, and an occasional shrillness of tone at odds with its ethos. It is rather too belligerent—too keen to show that it is not going to be pushed around. It is this that has made it acknowledge less than one would expect, its natural corollary and ally, altruism. The description of the human super-organism that emerges from the best (by which we mean the most radical) relational autonomy writing should *entail* altruism. If I acknowledge that the co-ordinates that describe my position in the universe are other humans, then a desire simply to persist and be locatable should mandate altruistic behaviour, at least in the limited sense of an outwardly directed, unself-regarding attention—which will bear the fruit of altruistic acts. We anticipate that as relational autonomy ages and acquires more confidence, it will more happily keep the company of altruism.

At times this chapter may have seemed to be too mystical for many appetites (and perhaps particularly for lawyers, who pride themselves on their hard-headed devotion to the facts). Talk of porous boundaries between individuals, and the melting of personality into the World Soul does not find its way readily into modern skeleton arguments in the law courts. So it is worth concluding with Derek Parfit, who, in his emphatic repudiation of mysticism in *Reasons and Persons,* comes to the same conclusions as the most ardent believer in the Communion of the Saints or the ecstatic *advaita* of Hindu mysticism. Part of the book is an argument for a type of impersonality.

> When we consider various imagined cases, we discover what we believe ourselves to be. Most of us believe that our identity must always be determinate. We believe that, to the question, 'Am I about to die?' there must always be an answer, which must be either and quite simply Yes or No.

> ….[T]his belief cannot be true unless persons are separately existing entities, distinct from their brains and bodies, and their experiences. The continued existence of these entities must be a deep, further fact, distinct from physical and psychological continuity, and a fact which either holds completely, or not at all. One such entity would be a Cartesian Ego. As our reactions to the imagined cases show, most of us are inclined to believe that we are such entities. I argued that this belief is false.
> Because this belief is false, we cannot explain the unity of a person's life by claiming that the experiences in this life are all had by this person. We can explain this unity only by describing the various relations that hold between these different experiences, and their relations to a particular brain. We could therefore describe a person's life in an impersonal way, which does not claim that this person exists.
> On this Reductionist View, persons do exist. But they exist only in the way in which nations exist. Persons are not, as we mistakenly believe, **fundamental.** This view is in this sense more impersonal (Parfit 1984, p. 445).

This conclusion is too radical for us, and for the law. But it is significant and salutary that so many traditions, travelling by very different routes, converge on a point whose location can be (inadequately) described as Communitarianism, and whose morality is altruism.

We accept entirely that morality and law should not be co-extensive. We are terribly frightened of theocracies—even secular ones. All that we have sought to demonstrate so far is that most serious thinkers have expressly rejected precisely that view of humans that the law so often takes granted.

But philosophy is just philosophy: it is just people's *views.* We now go on to argue, briefly, that there are some scientific grounds for saying that the philosophers we have quoted were right in their characterization of the quintessentially relational nature of humans, and in their conclusion that recognition of that relationality (supremely in altruism), is essential to human thriving.

2.9 Our Perception of What Makes Us Thrive

Happiness research is a rapidly expanding science. And while we can argue about whether what is meant by happiness is the same in all the studies (making comparisons of the studies difficult), and whether what is meant by happiness captures the holistic notion of thriving as Aristotle meant it (it doesn't, but there's certainly a good deal of overlap between 'happiness', however defined, and *eudaimonia*), the results are at least interesting, and sometimes very significant, for our purposes.

2.9.1 The Imperative of Authenticity

There is a very famous thought experiment, designed by Thomas Nozick (1974). He asks us to imagine that there is a machine which, if we are hooked up to it, can deliver the most pleasurable and desirable experiences that we can imagine. When we are hooked up, we cannot distinguish between real experiences and those induced by the machine. Very few of us would opt to be connected (Weijers 2013; Seligman and Pawelski 2003).

What does this indicate? It indicates, amongst other things, that there is a robust belief that there is more to life than mere personal pleasure or contentment, and that a life of unalloyed self-gratification is an unsatisfactory one. We all seem to think that we have a role; that we are actors in a play (interacting, and not just soliloquizing), that we have responsibilities to things other than our appetites, and that we have (the word is inescapable) a *purpose* that entails discharge of those responsibilities.

2.9.2 The Importance of Community Size

We are not very good at living in huge cities or working in huge organizations. Once the group to which we are affiliated grows beyond about 200 people, our unhappiness and dysfunctionality grows with the size of the group. There are many reasons for this, but one is no doubt that evolution didn't design us to deal with such numbers. We are still, constitutionally, hunter-gatherers, and groups of more than 200 just can't live successfully on the East African savanna: they eat their environment to destruction. Meaningful, co-operative relationships are literally vital to hunter-gatherers. They are poised all the time on the edge of a thermodynamic precipice, and they need to get on well with the other members of the group to avoid teetering over. The relationship part of our neurological software facilitates relationships with between 20 and 200 people. After that it starts to malfunction. In the bush that malfunction would manifest as feud, fracture and misery: in Manhattan it manifests as neurosis, loneliness and superficiality. This is another way of saying that we need not just bodies around us, but real relationships; passionate, committed mutuality.

2.9.3 Mirror Neurons

In 1990 an Italian neuroscientist, Vittorio Gallese, inserted an electrode into a single neurone in the premotor cortex of a monkey, and connected the electrode to an oscilloscope to monitor the electrical activity in the neurone. Gallese picked up a raisin. To his surprise, an impulse passed through the monkey's neurone. Why should that be? Then the monkey itself picked up a raisin, and an identical impulse was recorded.

Gallese had discovered mirror neurones. These are neurones that fire when we observe, hear, or even think of another person doing something. They are the reason why we feel fear when we're with the fearful, cry when we're with the tearful, and salivate when we see others eating. They're the neurones of empathy: they blur the frontier between us and others.

They make elusive the 'I' whose self-interest is the substrate of much of the law—and particularly of the 'best interests' test. The mirror neurone researcher Christian Keysers notes that *our brains are almost magically connected to each other. We are not born with a brain that deals exclusively with ourselves, but with one capable of feeling with other people. Our brain is set up to resonate with the people around us. In this light, my attitude toward my intuition[s] has changed. I used to consider them unreliable and inferior to my rational thoughts, but now I see them as the result of a very cunning and exquisitely evolved process that utilizes the richness of my own motor expertise to gain insights into other people. Intuition has become like a faithful collaborator for me. I do not have to control and steer her work but I can trust her conclusions....Before shared circuits, our vision of the brain was essentially individualistic...In [the] light of the new research, people around us are no longer just part of the 'world out there', restricted to sensory brain areas. Through shared circuits, the people around us, their actions and their emotions, permeate into many areas of our brain that were formerly the safe harbours of our identity: our motor system and our feelings. The border between individuals becomes permeable, and the social and the private world intermix. Emotions and actions are contagious. Invisible strings of shared circuits tie our minds together, creating the fabric of an organic system that goes beyond the individual* (Keysers 2011).

2.9.4 Being Religious

Being religious, wherever you are in the world, makes you (relatively) happy. Or, at any rate, people who say that they are religious say that they are happy. And, to a first approximation, the more religious they say they are, the happier they say they are (Gittins 2010, p. 54).

These sorts of results attract cynicism, typically along the lines of: 'They would say that wouldn't they? If they don't say that God makes them happy, they'll think that their God will punish them for ingratitude.' And there are indeed difficulties in interpreting the data. Yet the results are consistent, and hold even after controlling for factors such as income, age and marital status (Gittins 2010, p. 54). No doubt a conviction of eternal security and the possession of a scheme by which to answer ontologically troubling questions both contribute to the effect, but so, no doubt, does the strong association of religion with community and altruism. Religious institutions offer membership and support, particularly to those who have no other affiliation. As we will see, the process of offering support is likely to be even more therapeutic than the process of receiving it.

2.9.5 *Happy Personalities*

Four personality traits correlate well with being happy: self-esteem, control over one's own life choices, optimism, and, finally, extroversion (Shermer 2008).

It is this fourth trait that interests us. Extroverts like being with others; they draw energy from relationships, and pump energy into others. They are likely to acknowledge the porosity of their own boundaries. The studies indicate that it is good to be porous.

2.9.6 *The Happiness of Spending Money on Others*

As incomes rise, happiness does not: or not clearly. The mere possession of money, at any rate, does not make us happy (Gittins 2010, pp. 69–97). Some of the things that may be entailed in the possession of money (such as doing a satisfying, demanding job, or acquiring status) or made possible by money (such as the ability to avoid unhappy-making tasks), may promote happiness. Guzzling caviar, or buying expensive trinkets, certainly do not. Yet money can apparently buy happiness—if the money is spent on others. Thus if you contribute some of a bonus payment to someone else, you will enjoy the bonus more. The way in which the bonus is spent is a better predictor of the bonus-generated happiness than the size of the bonus (Dunn, Aknin and Norton 2008).

2.9.7 *Happiness and Work*

Our satisfaction with and happiness at work seems to be closely related to the relationality at work, and the perceived usefulness to others of the work. A 2007 survey (Smith 2007), found that amongst the top ten most satisfied with their jobs were clergy (number 1), physiotherapists (2), firefighters (3), educational administrators (4), teachers, (6), psychologists (8) and Special Education teachers (9). Amongst the ten least satisfied were the roofers, who found their jobs the least satisfying of all (1), waiters/servers (2), labourers (except construction) (3), bar tenders (4), hand packers and packagers (5), freight, stock and material handlers (6), apparel clothing salespersons (7), and cashiers (8). Satisfaction and happiness tracked each other to some extent: clergy were the happiest (1), followed by fire-fighters (2), and Special Education Teachers (5). The least happy were garage and service station attendants (1), the poor roofers (2), and moulding and casting machine operatives (3).

All of the jobs ranked high for satisfaction and happiness are helping, outward-looking jobs. They involve the abdication of self and the promotion of the interests of others. They are also, to a greater extent than many other jobs, jobs that involve association with and identification with a community or communities: clergy with their parishioners; firefighters with each other, bound in a common, heroic enterprise, and with those they rescue, teachers with their children and the children's parents, and so on.

The economic journalist Ross Gittins (2010, p. 117) suggests that even jobs that are 'simple or repetitive and have little meaningful purpose' can be made more satisfying:

> One way of doing it is to insert more people into them – to become more conscious of the people who are the end-beneficiaries of the work being performed, to have more contact with them or, if nothing else, have more fun with your workmates.
>
> Happiness psychologists like to tell the story of the creative hospital cleaner. In theory, your classic repetitive, unrewarding job. But not in the hands of this lady. She's very aware of the job she does in helping to combat hospital-borne germs and in keeping the place pleasant for patients, their relatives, doctors and nurses. She offers friendly chit-chat to all who come her way, rearranges the photos in patients' rooms to give them something new to look at and tries to clean those rooms at times most convenient to relatives.

2.9.8 Happiness, Health and Altruism

The hospital cleaner demonstrates a general principle, foreshadowed by the philosophers and the religions, that if you seek to gratify yourself you will fail, but if you seek to gratify others you will succeed not only in gratifying them but in gratifying yourself. Happiness, it seems, cannot be seized directly; it has to be seized indirectly, by seeking the happiness of others. The psychologists have given this principle a name: it is the 'teleological paradox'. Gittins illustrates it with a study in which students were asked to list the ten people they knew best, and say whether they considered each person (a) happy or unhappy and (b) selfish or unselfish. The students concluded that 95 % of the selfish people were unhappy, and 70 % of the unselfish ones were happy (Gittins 2010, p. 141).

Altruism doesn't just make you happy, it also makes you healthy. Volunteering one's time gratuitously is associated with significantly reduced mortality in both older (Brown and Brown 2006; Brown et al. 2003, 2008, 2009, 2011; Grimm, Spring and Dietz 2007; Harris and Thoresen 2005; Oman 2007; Oman, Thoresen and McMahon 1999; Luoh and Herzog 2002) and younger adults (Pillemer et al. 2010), reduced depression (Lum and Lightfoot 2005), and generally better physical and psychological functioning (Greenfield and Marks 2004; Piliavin and Siegl 2007; Pinquart and Sorensen 2003; Thoits and Hewitt 2001). The effects are dramatic. One example: giving time voluntarily to two or more organizations reduced mortality in people over 55 years by 44 % (after controlling for previous health status) (Oman, Thoresen and McMaho 1999).

Why should this be so? There has been no shortage of speculation. An obvious thought is that volunteering increases the number of social contacts, and that that increased relationality itself has health benefits. That was thought to be at least part of the story (Wilson and Musick 1999), and would have supported our contention that a human being alone is a human being who is not thriving. Yet there is more to it than that, as more finessed studies have shown. Volunteering confers more health benefits than merely social activities with a comparable number of social interactions (Piliavin and Siegl 2007). This seems to be because volunteering of a particular kind confers a sense of meaningfulness that mere sociability does not (Piliavin and Siegl 2007), and/or avoids a sense of meaninglessness that mere sociability, without more, can tend to generate (Musick, Herzog and House 1999). Yet what 'particular kind' are we talking about? The evidence about that is new, but clear. Volunteering per se does not increase your longevity: volunteers live longer than non-volunteers if, and only if, they volunteer for 'other-oriented' reasons (Konrath et al. 2012). It is altruism, not chatter, that is good for you.

2.10 Conclusion

C.S. Lewis (1940) wrote that 'The golden apple of selfhood, thrown among the false gods, became an apple of discord because they scrambled for it. They did not know the first rule of the holy game, which is that every player must by all means touch the ball and then immediately pass it on. To be found with it in your hands is a fault: to cling to it, death.'

Lewis, and the Greeks to whose myth he was referring,[3] meant this to be a metaphysical parable, but it seems that it may be literally, physiologically, anatomically true too. It is not surprising. There is no clear boundary between our minds, souls and bodies, any more than there is a clear boundary between ourselves and our neighbours.

References

Aristotle Nichomachean Ethics 8(1) (trans: Ross WD). www.classics.mit.edu

Ashton MC, Paunonen SV, Helmes E, Jackson DN (1998) Kin altruism, reciprocal altruism, and the Big Five personality factors. Evol Hum Behav 19(4):243–255

Aurelius M (1946) Meditations (trans: Staniforth M). Penguin, London

Bentham J (1776) A fragment on government. London

Berenson F (1982) Hegel on others and the self. Philosophy 57:77–90

Bierwiler K (1978) Pitirim Sorokin's research in altruism. State University of New York, Albany

Brown SL, Brown RM (2006) Selective investment theory: recasting the functional significance of close relationships. Psychol Inq 17:1–29

[3]It is a reference to the golden apple on which the goddess Eris inscribed 'to the fairest'. She then threw it amongst the divine revellers at a wedding. Their scrambling for it eventually led to the Trojan War.

Brown S, Nesse R, Vinokur AD, Smith DM (2003) Providing support may be more beneficial than receiving it: results from a prospective study of mortality. Psychol Sci 14:320–327
Brown SL, Brown RM, House JS, Smith DM (2008) Coping with spousal loss: the potential buffering effects of self-reported helping behavior. Personal Soc Psychol Bull 34:849–861
Brown SL, Smith DM, Schulz R, Kabeto M, Ubel P, Yee J, Langa K (2009) Caregiving and decreased mortality in a national sample of older adults. Psychol Sci 20:488–494
Brown SL, Brown RM, Preston S (2011) A model of human caregiving motivation. In: Brown S, Brown R, Penner S (eds) Moving beyond self interest: perspectives from evolutionary biology, neuroscience, and the social sciences. Oxford University Press, New York
Comte A (1891) Catechism of positivism (trans: Congreve R). Kegan Paul, London
Comte A (1973) System of positive polity, volume 1: containing the general view of positivism and introductory principles (trans: Bridges JH). Burt Franklin, New York
Dunn EW, Aknin LB, Norton MI (2008) Spending money on others promotes happiness. Science 319(5870):1687–1688
Durkheim E (1973) Moral education: a study in the theory and application of the sociology of education. The Free Press, London
Eberhard MJW (1975) The evolution of social behavior by kin selection. Quart Rev Biol 50:1–33
Foster KR, Wenseleers T, Ratnieks FL (2006) Kin selection is the key to altruism. Trends Ecol Evol 21(2):57–60
Gittins R (2010) The happy economist: happiness for the hard-headed. Allen & Unwin, Crows Nest, NSW
Golub C (2014) Altruism: a natural thought history of an idea. Wellesley College, Honors Thesis Collection. Paper 190
Grayling AC (2011) What is good?. Hachette, London
Greenfield EA, Marks NF (2004) Formal volunteering as a protective factor for older adults' psychological well-being. J Gerontol Ser B 59:S258–S266
Grimm R, Spring K, Dietz N (2007) The health benefits of volunteering: a review of recent research. Corporation for National & Community Service, New York
Haldane JB (1926) On being the right size. Harper's Magazine 152:424–427
Harris AH, Thoresen CE (2005) Volunteering is associated with delayed mortality in older people: analysis of the longitudinal study of aging. J Health Psychol 10:739–752
Jaynes J (2000) The origin of consciousness in the breakdown of the bicameral mind. Houghton Mifflin Harcourt, Boston, MA
Keysers C (2011) The empathic brain. Createspace, New York
Konrath S, Fuhrel-Forbis A, Lou A, Brown S (2012) Motives for volunteering are associated with mortality risk in older adults. Health Psychol 31(1):87–95
Kropotkin P (1910) Mutual aid: a factor of evolution. Free Press, London
Lewis CS (1940) The problem of pain. Geoffrey Bles, London
Lum TY, Lightfoot E (2005) The effects of volunteering on the physical and mental health of older people. Res Aging 27:31–55
Luoh M-C, Herzog AR (2002) Individual consequences of volunteer and paid work in old age: health and mortality. J Health Soc Behav 43:490–509
Mill JS (1906) Utilitarianism. University of Chicago Press, Chicago
Musick M, Herzog AR, House JS (1999) Volunteering and mortality among older adults: findings from a national sample. J Gerontol Ser B: Psychol Sci Soc Sci 54:S173–S 175
Nozick R (1974) Anarchy, state, and utopia. Basic Books, New York
Oman D (2007) Does volunteering foster physical health and longevity? In: Post SG (ed) Altruism and health: perspectives from empirical research. Oxford University Press, New York, pp 15–32
Oman D, Thoresen CE, McMahon K (1999) Volunteerism and mortality among the community dwelling elderly. J Health Psychol 4:301–316
Parfit D (1984) Reasons and persons. Clarendon Press, Oxford
Piliavin JA, Siegl E (2007) Health benefits of volunteering in the Wisconsin Longitudinal Study. J Health Soc Behav 48:450–464

Pillemer K, Fuller-Rowell TE, Reid MC, Wells NM (2010) Environmental volunteering and health outcomes over a 20-year period. The Gerontologist 50:594–602
Pinquart M, Sorensen S (2003) Differences between caregivers and non-caregivers in psychological health and physical health: a meta-analysis. Psychol Aging 18:250–267
Savulescu J (2014) Why I am not a utilitarian. http://blog.practicalethics.ox.ac.uk/2014/11/why-i-am-not-a-utilitarian/. Accessed 18 March 2015
Seligman ME, Pawelski J (2003) Positive psychology: FAQS. Psychol Inquiry 159–163
Shermer M (2008) The mind of the market: compassionate apes, competitive humans, and other tales from evolutionary economics. Macmillan, London
Smith JM (1964) Group selection and kin selection. Nature 201:1145–1147
Smith T (2007) Job satisfaction in the United States: America's general social survey: national opinion research Centre. University of Chicago, Chicago
Sorokin P (1954) Forms and techniques of altruistic and spiritual growth. Beacon Press, Boston
Spencer H (1879) The data of ethics. Hurst, New York
Thoits PA, Hewitt LN (2001) Volunteer work and well-being. J Health Soc Behav 42:115–131
Trivers RL (1971) The evolution of reciprocal altruism. Quart Rev Biol 46:35–57
Weijers D (2013) Intuitive biases in judgments about thought experiments: the experience machine revisited. Philos Writ 41(1):17–31
West R (1997) Caring for justice. New York University Press, New York
Wilkinson GS (1988) Reciprocal altruism in bats and other mammals. Ethol Sociobiol 9(2):85–100
Wilson DS (1975) A theory of group selection. Proc Natl Acad Sci USA 72(1):143–146
Wilson J, Musick M (1999) The effects of volunteering on the volunteer. Law Contemp Probl 62:141–168
Wilson DS, Sober E (1994) Reintroducing group selection to the human behavioral sciences. Behav Brain Sci 17(4):585–608

Chapter 3
Rethinking the Welfare and Best Interest Principles

Abstract This chapter explores the legal principles of welfare and best interests. It argues that these terms are not properly understood in individualistic terms but are, or at least should be, characterised by mutual respect, by the acceptance of responsibility for others, and by an acknowledgement of our intrinsic, defining interrelationality. It considers some of the criticisms that have been levelled against relational understandings of welfare and best interests, and finds them unconvincing.

Keywords Best interests · Welfare · Responsibility · Domestic abuse · Autonomy

3.1 Introduction

We now move to the world of the court room. What is the relevance of all the discussion so far in this book to judges making actual decisions? Altruism and community, we suggest, become particularly significant when the courts are making decisions for those unable to make decisions for themselves. These are, essentially, cases involving children and those lacking mental capacity. It is then that the notions of welfare and best interests come on to the centre of the forensic stage.

In this chapter we outline how a court, adopting the arguments made in the first half of this book, should interpret welfare and best interests principles. In the next chapter we argue that, in fact, the conclusions reached by the courts in many cases are entirely consistent with our approach. In other words we are not arguing for the courts to take a radical change in direction, but rather are providing them with a theoretical justification for the results they are already reaching, and encouraging them to continue in this direction.

The problem with judicial statements on welfare and best interests is that, as Munby LJ (2010, p. 548) (writing extra-judicially) has put it:

> What exactly is meant by a patient's best interests is neither self-evident nor altogether clear. There are two reasons for this uncertainty. First, the question has been given

C. Foster and J. Herring, *Altruism, Welfare and the Law*,
SpringerBriefs in Law, DOI 10.1007/978-3-319-21605-8_3

> surprisingly little consideration by the courts. Secondly, and not-withstanding strong criticism, the courts have traditionally failed, and even on occasions refused, to articulate any principles or values to be applied in operating the best interests test.

This chapter explains how the courts can still uphold the best interests or welfare tests, while taking into account the individual's relations with others and the well-being of those close to them, the obligations they have, and the need for virtue.

3.2 An Overarching Theme: Relational Best Interests

Writing in the context of children, one of us (Jonathan Herring) has argued in favour of an approach he calls "relationship-based welfare". This approach claims that children are best raised in the context of healthy relationships. Legal responses to disputes should be seen in the context of those relationships and should promote good relationships for children and free them from harmful ones. Central to this understanding is that healthy relationships involve a fair degree of give and take between the family members. As a result, it is neither appropriate nor possible to take every decision based simply on what will promote the interests of one particular child at one particular time. Anyone who has lived in a family knows that there are times when, quite properly, a decision is made which will not be best for one member (if their interests were somehow considered in isolation) but will promote the good of the whole family. Any family that has more than one child will know that inevitably the interests of children compete. One day a decision will be made which (seen in an artificially isolated way) appears to promote the interests of one child over the others; another day the interests of a different child will seem to prevail. Similarly, parents have their own lives to lead and cannot constantly "put their children's interests before their own".[1] That is not, of course, to harm the children. It promotes the welfare of a child to be in a family which considers the interest of all the family members (Sevenhuijsen 2003). It would not be in a child's overall welfare interests for every decision pertaining to the child to be made solely on the grounds of that child's best interests, when those best interests are assessed atomistically. Spoilt brats are not happy. Few of us—at least with the benefit of hindsight—would want to be raised in that way. Few of us raise children that way.

Barbara Bennett Woodhouse (1993, p. 1825) has explained:

> A truly child-centred perspective would also expose the fallacy that children can thrive while their care givers struggle, or that the care giver's needs can be severed from the child's, which has led to the attitude that violence, hostility, and neglect toward the care giver are somehow irrelevant in the best interest calculus.

The same point can be made in the context of caring relationships with adults lacking capacity. Such relationships also should involve give and take. The job of a

[1] Our argument is, that this way of looking at the issue, separating out the interests of parents and children, cannot be done. But we use language to clarify the point we are making.

carer, hard enough as it is, would become impossible if every decision had to be made based solely on the other's needs. Few if any of us would want, were we to lose capacity, to have our families, or even employed carers, making every decision based solely on our interests, with no thought for themselves. We would not want them making huge sacrifices in an attempt to improve our welfare marginally.

Promoting welfare and best interests means, therefore, promoting good relationships. It means considering what is the right decision in the context of the relationship between the parties. It means recognizing the responsibilities that can flow from relationships. It means ensuring that children, those lacking capacity, and indeed everyone, can live in relationships that promote their flourishing.

Let's unpack some of these ideas a little further in considering how relational welfare or best interests can be put into practice.

3.3 Autonomy, Interdependence and Vulnerability

A key question a judge will inevitably ask when making a welfare or best interests assessment is: "what result am I aiming for in the long term?" A prominent view in relation to children is that the goal is autonomy. When making decisions about children we should be seeking to enable them to reach adulthood with a maximum level of capacity.

To examine this more closely, we look at the approach to children's rights and interests promoted by John Eekelaar. In his seminal writings on children's rights, he says that the goal of the law on children is: 'To bring children to the threshold of adulthood with the maximum opportunities to form and pursue life-goals which reflect as closely as possible an autonomous choice' (Eekelaar 1994, p. 53). To achieve this goal: 'in making decisions about children's upbringing, care should be taken to avoid imposing inflexible outcomes at an early stage in a child's development which unduly limit the child's capacity to fashion his/her own identity, and the context in which it flourishes best' (Eekelaar 1994, p. 55). As a result he supports allowing children to make decisions for themselves, unless doing so would infringe one or more or their important interests (what he describes as basic or developmental interests). This system allows children to gain the skills of decision-making, but never at the expense of causing them serious harm (which harm would limit the range of options they would have when they reached full autonomy at adulthood.)

A detailed consideration of Eekelaar's view is beyond the scope of this book: it would entail an examination of the nature of children's rights. We acknowledge that there is much to commend in his view. However, we question the desired outcome of his approach: a child which has the maximal capacity for autonomous living. Autonomy is not the only ability we would wish our children to have. We value a much broader range of abilities. These include: the ability to form and maintain relationships; to have a proper sense of obligation; to have respect for others; to be fun to be with; to be excited by the new, and so on. A crucial part of children developing with these skills is teaching them what it means to be part of a family, a community or group of friends. That means realizing that you cannot have your way on every issue; that the good of families and communities is found by taking the interests of all the members into account. It is true that in families the interests of children should be the focus of the family's attention, but children should learn what it means to be part of a communal enterprise. That family life involves give and take, and accordingly one's obligations to others mean that one cannot simply do as one pleases. It is, therefore, not in a child's best interests for every decision relating to him or her be made on the narrow basis of the child's happiness. Children should not only be autonomous, but also kind, responsible, adventurous and quirky—to name but a few qualities. Schools see it as a central part of their mission to instill values, citizenship and a sense of responsibility. The law should too. And we argue there is nothing in the welfare principle or the best interests test that would stop a court from doing that. Indeed quite the opposite: we say that the law requires it.

We suggest that the inappropriate emphasis on autonomy as the goal for our children explains some repercussively negative comments about childhood. David Archard (2001, p. 52) has written:

> There may be features of childhood but not of adulthood which are valuable, such as innocence, wonder and trust. There may, correspondingly be features of adulthood but not childhood which are valuable, such as experience and independence. It is also evident that there may be features of childhood but not of adulthood which are not valuable, such as dependence and vulnerability.

We think both of these views are profoundly mistaken. Vulnerability and dependence are not only inevitable parts of humanity, as argued earlier in this book, but they are virtues, not vices, without which we are not optimally thriving.

An approach which seeks to promote the welfare of the child in the abstract, rather than locating the child in her relational context, is flawed, because we cannot understand the wellbeing of one person in an intimate caring relationship in isolation from the wellbeing of others. In caring relationships, what is good for one party is good for another. That is why people like to celebrate with their friends or family members when good things happen to them. Good news for them is good news for us. The same is true for communal commiseration when bad things happens. A child's illness affects the plans of the whole family. The cheerful mood of the toddler infects those around her with her sense of fun. Seeking to promote "just" the welfare of the child or adult lacking capacity makes no sense when lives are so intertwined and our identities so merged (Shakespeare 2000). In intimate relationships, we do not break down into 'me' and 'you' (Clement 1996, p. 11).

Many of these points can be made in relation to those lacking capacity for reasons other than age. Of course, there is a fundamental difference in that while it is plausible to look forward to a time of autonomy for most children, that is not possible for many adults with capacity that is not possible.[2] The path ahead for many is ever decreasing decision-making ability. Yet still, for such patients, maximising autonomy is a central criterion in determining the decisions that can lawfully be made. A finding of incapacity requires clear evidence. The courts are more fearful of treating a capacitous person as incapacitous than they are of treating an incapacitous person as capacitous. See, for example, the decision in *PC v York CC* where a young woman formed a relationship with a man with a history of violence against women. She had a low IQ and was vulnerable. While accepting the unanimous professional opinion that he posed a serious risk to her and that PC was a vulnerable young woman, the Court of Appeal overturned the first instance decision that she lacked capacity to make the decision to cohabit and ruled:

> There may be many women who are seen to be in relationships with men regarded by professionals as predatory sexual offenders. The Court of Protection does not have jurisdiction to act to 'protect' these women if they do not lack the mental capacity to decide whether or not to be, or continue to be, in such a relationship. … The statute respects their autonomy so to decide and the Court of Protection has no jurisdiction to intervene.

This approach (rightly) emphasises the importance of autonomy for adults, but it can be questioned (Herring and Wall 2014). Susan Dodds (2007, p. 507) has argued that it is important to recognise vulnerability:

> A vulnerability-centered view of the self and of persons is better able to capture more of our moral motivations and intuitions than can be captured by an autonomy-focused approach. We are all vulnerable to the exigencies of our embodied, social and relational existence and in recognizing this inherent human vulnerability, we can see the ways in which a range of social institutions and structures protect us against some vulnerabilities, while others expose us to risk. We do not have to view our obligations towards those who lack the capacity to develop or retain autonomy as having a different source from our obligations towards those whose autonomy is made vulnerable due to a degree of dependency. It may be easier to recognize the social value of provision of care if it is viewed as something on which we all have been dependent and on which we are all likely to be dependent at different points in our lives, rather than altruistic behaviour extended to those who lack 'full personhood.'

Whether in the case of lone parents, or care in the community for incapacitous adults, autonomy and independence have become key policy goals, regardless of a person's capacity. But this ignores the fact that as humans we are interdependent (Dodds 2005). No one can be truly independent. We need to recognise the benefits of vulnerability. Janine Wiles (2011, p. 573) writes:

> Vulnerability is often seen as fragility or weakness, but it may also be conceptualised as openness, susceptibility, and receptiveness. Ideas about vulnerability as inherent to the self and as formative might be usefully applied to the experiences of older care recipients. To experience and acknowledge one's vulnerability may be a process of renegotiation of one's sense of embodied self and relationships to people and places.

---

[2] The extent to which a person without capacity can meaningfully exercise autonomy at all is a question we put to one side for the moment.

Our best interests and welfare are not served by severing us from our responsibilities and our relationships so as to be free to live our lives as we wish. Assessments of best interests must acknowledge that it is our human nature to be vulnerable and to be sustained through our relationships with others. No one can seek to promote their own interests in isolation from the interests of others.

So: the model we advocate, both for children and adults, is not one that seeks simply to produce merely autonomous individuals. Instead, our goal must be to promote the thriving of individuals in a network of caring relationships which works for the good of all. This recognises that, alone, we cannot be what we want to be. We become more ourselves (and therefore acquire an *us* which can thrive) by embedding our lives in the lives of others. Our caring relationships and responsibilities with others are not merely ties that bind, but are tools to promote our flourishing. We want children who value their relationships, recognise their dependence on others, and rejoice in their obligation, not children free of all ties who have the autonomy to choose to be (unnaturally, unthrivingly) alone, free as the untethered balloon in the wind, and about as useful.

3.4 Understanding a Good Relationship

So, the our goal for courts making decisions for those who cannot make decisions for themselves is same as it is for anyone—namely that they live in good relationships. But, what exactly do we mean by a good relationship? The answer, in short, is a caring relationship. The literature about the ethics of care can help us to understand what this means (Gilligan 1982; Tronto 1983; Sevenhuijsen 1998; Groenhout 2004; Held 2006; Engster 2007; Bridgeman 2009; Herring 2013).

Before going any further, we emphasise that we are using the terminology of *caring relationships*. Too often in the care literature there is a marked separation between the "carer" and the "cared for". This carries all kinds of dangers—not least in tending to disempower the "cared for", and viewing care as a uni-directional activity. The reality is that relationships involving children and adults lacking capacity are multi-directional. All parents are cared for by their children. Parents learn from their children, receive emotional support from them, and are uplifted in truly remarkable ways. Those who care for adults with severe impairments become aware of extrarordinary openness, spontaneity, joy, and generosity. This is not to pretend that childhood and impairment are not sometimes difficult and challenging. But so too are adulthood and "normality", (whatever that means). Janet Fink (2004, p. 14) has written of the dangers of writing about disabled people without listening to the experiences of families:

> First, it has perpetuated the continuing tendency of discourses of care to constitute disabled people as an inevitable burden on their families, thereby setting up a dichotomy between 'normal' families and families with disabled members. This suggests that one set of relationships is benign and 'the other is problematic and pathological'. Second, it has elided the ways in which care relationships can be understood as being built around elements of

> reciprocity and interdependence, failing, thereby, to acknowledge that in some places and at some times, we have all experienced giving and receiving care.

It is important, then, to recognise that in talking about children and those lacking capacity, it is not a matter of parents caring for children or "carers" looking after the "disabled" (Herring 2014b). Rather there are rich, intermingled, interdependent relationships—just as happens whenever any humans truly relate to each other.

So: what are the features of a caring relationship? We suggest that there are four.

3.4.1 Meeting Needs

Caring relationships meet needs. Care is not just a feeling: it is not just caring *about* someone. It is caring *for* them (Miller 2005). The focus should not be on the emotions that people have, or claim to have, but rather on the activities of caring they engage in (Tronto 1983, pp. 127–134). This is why a parent seeking to justify having a stake in a child's well-being needs to do more than claim they have feelings towards their child, and needs to show they are actively involved in the child's life. Quite rightly the European Court of Human Rights has held that a parent seeking an enforceable right to respect for family life in relation to a child needs more than simply a biological link. By your fruits you shall know them: failure to act in the face of need casts doubt on the claim to have a caring attitude.

3.4.2 Respect

Respect is key to care. Respect involves being alert to the needs of the other, and responding to that person as an individual, in a way appropriate to them. One should not treat the person as an "object" with a need, but determine what is appropriate in the context of ones relationship with them. Robin Dillon (1992, p. 128) captures this in the word 'attention' and argues:

> The term 'care' denotes here an epistemic attitude, understood as a moral ideal of attention: a commitment to attend, with intensely focused perception to all aspects of the irreducible particularity of individual human persons in their concrete contexts.

Respect requires a degree of empathy and anticipation. It involves imagining how the other would like her needs to be met, and listening to her. It requires accepting that what most people might want in a particular case is not necessarily what the individual necessarily wants. It also entails treating a person in a dignified way and respecting their innate humanity. This is likely to involve undertaking intimate aspects of care sensitively and privately, and allowing the individual to do for themselves what thy can do. This can involve appreciating how the person understands the nature of and justification for the care (Engster 2007, p. 55). Crucially it requires both parties to the relationship to be respectful of each other.

3.4.3 Responsibility

The best kind of care involves an assumption of responsibility. Caring for another only when it is convenient to do so is not the best kind of care. Caring should not be seen as the tick-box performance of tasks. It about relationships which entail responsibilities.

3.4.4 Relationality

As already discussed, caring should be relational. Both parties to the relationship should be open to receiving care as well as giving it (Dalmiya 2002). There is an important contrast between an approach based on 'activity caring' and one based on 'relational caring'. The activity-based approach to care is likely to understand caring as involving 'doing something for someone else' (Ungerson 1990). This is a (sometimes dangerously) narrow view of caring. It differentiates, inappropriately, between the roles of 'carer' and 'cared for'. Relational care, by contrast, is described by Carol Gilligan (1982, p. 73) in this way:

> The ideal of care is thus an activity of relationships, of seeing and responding to need, taking care of the world by sustaining the web of connection so that no one is left alone. Consider the following comment from a woman about using her husband, Andy, as a 'carer': I prefer to have Andy's help as a caregiver as little as possible, simply because if your husband becomes your caregiver, then he isn't your husband any more. The relationship is blurred there. If I still want to be a person unto myself, then I don't want to include him in some parts of care, like a bowel treatment or a shower day (quoted in England and Dyck 2011, p. 206).

This quotation highlights the fact that activities of care can take on different meanings, depending on the relationship between the parties. Here, because of their relationship, the most caring thing was for Andy *not* to undertake some tasks.

3.5 The Nature and Significance of Abuse

We have just outlined what caring relationships are like. We have also, throughout the book, explained the benefit of good relations. This is important because it helps to establish what we are seeking to achieve when we assess welfare or best interests. But there is another very important aspect: it is only through appreciating what truly caring relationships are that we can see why abuse is so harmful—and indeed why abuse in the sphere of intimate relations is even more serious than abuse in other contexts (Herring 2011).

From our earliest days our character and understanding of ourselves are fixed by and through relationships with others (Carle 2005). The value, then of relationships lies not simply in the goods they produce, but in their identity-forming characteristics. John Eekelaar (2006) has argued that trust is at the heart of the intimacy, and that trust enables love and autonomy to develop. It is in being able to be completely honest and vulnerable with a partner that relationships can deepen, an understanding of self can grow, and sense can be made of life. All of that depends on trust. In cases of domestic violence and child abuse the abuse is misuse of the intimate sphere. There are three forms of that misuse we wish to emphasise.

First: an intimate relationship involves "thick interpersonal trust" (Khodyakov 2007), which involves the disclosing of parts of ourselves (both physical and emotional) that we would normally wish to keep free from others. The kind of openness necessary for intimacy is so extensive that there are particularly strong bonds of trust. The trust involves an obligation not to use the relationship to take advantage of the other person. The relationship between carer/parent and child is particularly close. No one trusts like a young child—a child lacking the knowledge that trust can be misplaced and that those whom you love can hurt you the most. Both society and the child place on the parent/carer the obligations inherent in this type of trust. Domestic and child abuse can involve the use of information gathered during the relationship so as to personalise the abuse (Attorney-General's Reference (No 90 of 2009) (2009); Herring 2011).

Second: the abuse of trust within an intimate relationship causes especial harm. Intimate relationships are central to our identity and sense of self (Rachmilovitz 2007). Within our intimate relationships we can be truly ourselves, free of pretence. Through them, we can explore and discover ourselves. Children's relationships with their parents/primary carers are central to their identity. The long term impact of parental abuse on children is well documented. Domestic abuse strikes at the victim's very conception of the self. As Evan Stark (2007, p. 363) writes:

> In the romantic vernacular, love and intimacy compensate women for their devaluation in the wider world. Personal life does something more. It provides the state where women practice their basic rights, garner the support needed to resist devaluation, experiment with sexual identities, and imagine themselves through various life projects. Coercive control subverts this process, brining discrimination home by reducing the discretion in everyday routines to near zero, freezing feeling and identity in time and space, the process victims experience as entrapment. Extended across the range of activities that define women as person, this foreshortening of subjective development compounds the particular liberty harms caused by coercive control.

Child abuse and abuse in caring relationships turn what should be a tool for self-affirmation and self-identification into a tool for alienation and self-betrayal. The victim almost becomes used as a tool against herself (Arnault 2003). It is not surprising, therefore, that domestic violence causes a wide range of mental health problems for victims, ranging from anxiety and depression to post-traumatic stress, substance abuse and suicidal tendencies (Itzen et al. 2010). The relationships which should give the child a sense of self worth, a knowledge of being loved and lovable, and a realisation of the value of living in community with others, are turned to destroy the child's awareness of their value and to generate fear of intimacy with others. An atomised understanding of welfare or best interests fails to capture the true nature of the wrong of intimate abuse.

3.6 The Importance of Taking the Longer View

We now turn to another consequence of taking the relational and virtue-based approach to welfare. This is that welfare/best interests can only be understood by examining the network of relationships within which the individual lives, and this in turn involves looking both back to the past and forward to the future. There is a danger in making a welfare or best interests assessment focus on the particular question that is brought to the court, such as 'should this child attend this school?' or 'should this person be moved to a care home?' As we shall see in the next chapter, in deciding such questions the court typically encourages the use of a "checklist". This sets out the pros and cons of the proposed course of action. The judge then has the task of weighing these up to reach a considered conclusion. However, such an approach neglects the broader relational context of the decision. It fails to look back at the evolution of the relevant relationships, and at the obligations that may flow from what has happened. It can also fail to look at what may be required of the parties in the times ahead. We need to view the welfare/best interests decision in the context of what has been and of what is to come—in short, holistically, and within the relational context.

The court should make decisions in the same way that people actually make decisions in the context of intimate relationships. We do not see our personal lives as constantly involving clashes of individual rights or interests, but rather as a working out of relationships (Bridgeman 2009). The muddled give and take of everyday caring life, where sacrifices are made and benefits gained, without them being totted up on some giant familial star chart, chimes more with everyday life than the image of independent interests and rights. The man looking after his demented mother is not carefully adding up the pounds and hours to ensure that her rights are protected. The question is whether the relationship, looked at from all angles, is generally marked by fairness and reciprocity. To consider each issue in isolation is to risk distortion. In relationships the interests and well-being of two or more people become merged. As Diana Meyers (2004, p. 299) puts it, the self:

> is the interpersonally bounded self…As relational selves…people share in one another's joys and sorrows, give and receive care, and generally profit from the many rewards and cope with the many aggravations of friendship, family membership, religious or ethnic affiliation, and the like. These relationships are sources of moral identity, for people become committed to their intimates and to others whom they care about, and these commitments become central moral concerns

To develop this point further it may be helpful to consider a typical family law case. A child is living with the mother. Should the father have regular contact with the child? Under our approach, what questions would be relevant?

First, the current relationship between the child and father is a key factor. The closer the existing relationship between child and father, the stronger the argument for on-going contact. This is why talk of a "right to contact" for fathers is misguided. It somehow suggests that all child-father relationships can be described in terms of one right. The claim of a father who has a strong relationship with the child, where the child's sense of self is bound up with her father, has a very strong case for that relationship continuing in the most effective way possible. A father who has had no input into the child's life has a far weaker claim. So we need to move away from talking of a presumption in favour of contact with the father, or a right of contact with fathers, to look at the particular relationship in question (Herring 2014c).

Second, the network of family relationships needs to be considered. A contact claim is not simply a matter of a father's rights. The impact of contact or non-contact upon both parents and the child must be taken into account. The responsibilities generated by the relationships are an important factor. MacFarlane LJ was correct to comment in *Re W (contact)* (2012, para 55)

> In all aspects of life, whilst some duties and responsibilities may be a pleasure to discharge, others may well be unwelcome and a burden. Whilst parenting in many respects brings joy, even in families where life is comparatively harmonious, the responsibility of being a parent can be tough. Where parents separate the burden for each and every member of the family group can be, and probably will be, heavy. It is not easy, indeed it is tough, to be a single parent with the care of a child. Equally, it is tough to be the parent of a child for whom you no longer have the day to day care and with whom you no longer enjoy the ordinary stuff of everyday life because you only spend limited time with your child. Where all contact between a parent and a child is prevented, the burden on that parent will be of the highest order. Equally, for the parent who has the primary care of a child, to send that child off to spend time with the other parent may, in some cases, be itself a significant burden; it may, to use modern parlance, be "a very big ask". Where, however, it is plainly in the best interests of a child to spend time with the other parent then, tough or not, part of the responsibility of the parent with care must be the duty and responsibility to deliver what the child needs, hard though that may be.

But this argument works both ways. Abuse by the father of the mother will impact upon the child. We cannot view his relationship with the child in isolation from his behaviour towards the mother. To say that a father has been violent to the mother, but caring towards the child (as was suggested in *Re J-S (Contact Parental Responsibility)* (2002)) is a contradiction in terms. To harm a child's primary carer is to harm the child.

Third, particularly in the case of younger children, legal interventions 'run through the caregiver or caregivers' (Czapanskiy 1999). Contact between a parent and child can succeed only if there is a degree of willingness on the party of the other parent to support, or at least not disrupt, that relationship. Respect between the parents is key if contact is to succeed. Contact which is used to undermine the other parent or which seeks to destablise the child's other relationships will not promote a child's well-being.

Finally, it is essential to appreciate that it is not the existence of contact, nor even the length of time of contact which is important, but the quality of that contact and the quality of the relationship which emerges from it. Saying that a set number of hours or a set percentage of time is for the welfare of the child (whereas less or more is not) is artificial: it sees the litigation as a fight over a neatly divisible cake. The goal should be contact that will promote good relationships over time.

A good example of a judicial failure to take a broader look at a case is, we suggest, seen in *Re S* (*A Child*) (2002). This involved Victoria, who was nine and a half years old, and had Down's Syndrome. She had mild learning difficulties and a range of other medical problems. She needed extensive care. Her parents had separated when she was 18 months old, and later divorced. She lived with her mother in south London, but had weekly contact with her father, who lived nearby and had remarried. The mother had met a new partner, who lived in Cornwall. The new partner had an elderly mother who was dependent on him and lived nearby in Cornwall. The mother wished to move to Cornwall, but the father sought an order requiring her to remain in London. He emphasised that it was a 7 h journey between London and Cornwall, and that the move would therefore impact on the contact arrangements.

The question for the court was whether compelling her mother to remain in London would promote Victoria's welfare. The Court of Appeal emphasised that the interests of the mother were not relevant, save in so far as they directly impacted on Victoria's welfare. The court relied on expert evidence showing that Victoria would find the reduction in contact with the father confusing and distressing. It was, therefore, in her best interests to remain in London.

The difficulty with this decision is that it focused entirely on what was in Victoria's best interests at the time of the hearing. It failed to look at the longer timescale. This was a girl with considerable needs who had been given continuous intense care by her mother and would continue to receive that level of care for the rest of her life. The sacrifices made by her mother were enormous. The father had been free to remarry and, for most of the week, was free of the responsibilities of care. The mother had not had this freedom. The father was seeking to deny the mother the practical and emotional support that the new partner offered. It is hard to see how, looking at this issue in the context of the relationships between the parties, this order promoted Victoria's welfare.

3.7 The Importance of Responsibilities

A central part of relationships is the fact they bring responsibilities. Indeed we referred to responsibilities being a hallmark of a caring relationship. However, to many it seems odd to regard responsibilities as beneficial. Responsibilities are seen as restrictions on our autonomy—as a regrettable limitation on our rights. We should not, many say, "impose" responsibilities on children or those lacking capacity. However, we should remember that we begin our lives in relationships, and relationships are central to our lives. And with relationships come responsibilities. That is why it wrong to see us starting life as free and only subsequently 'burdened' by the responsibilities that we choose to assume. It is wrong to start with the question: "do I have the right to do X?" rather than: "What are my responsibilities in the context of this relationship" (Leckey 2007). As Polona Curk (2011, p. 51) puts it: "We take responsibility for each other because we continue to need each other and because we establish meaningful relationships through taking responsibility for each other." Parenthood is a good example of this. One cannot escape the responsibilities of parenthood by claiming one did not choose to be a parent, or of childhood, by claiming that one did not choose to be a child. Once it is appreciated that responsibilities are not chosen, but flow from relationships, there is no difficulty in acknowledging that children and those lacking capacity can have obligations to those in caring relationships with them. Children often say "I did not choose to be born"; but if relationships do not flow from choice, that is beside the point. The responsibilities of a relationship must be recognised to enable the relationship work and flourish. We have somehow twisted our moral sense by seeing responsibilities as emerging from rights. We should begin with our responsibilities and see rights as tools enabling us to fulfil our responsibilities (Held 2006; Williams 2002). Relationships and responsibilities, not rights and freedoms, are the reality of life for most people. Our lives are not characterised (thank goodness) by freedom and autonomy. Rather it is in seeking to meet our responsibilities to others in the context of our defining relationships that enables us to flourish. This is as true for those lacking capacity as it is anyone else.

3.8 The Importance of Looking at the Particular Case

If a court is to take a relational approach it must focus on the particular individuals and their relationships. The welfare principle and best interests test should not be restricted to a set of abstract moral rules. Instead of starting with a series of "thou shalt nots", we should start with the context and concrete reality of the particular situations, the individuals and their relationships. What might work for one group of people in one situation will not work for another group in a different situation. Hence it is that relational ethics will often make remarks such as, 'well: it all depends on the circumstances of the case'. That is because it does. Nel Noddings (1984, p. 5) writes:

> Since so much depends on the subjective experience of those involved in ethical encounters, conditions are rarely 'sufficiently similar' for me to declare that you must do what I must do

This is one of the problems with presumptions. They tend to be based on crude generalisations about what is best for children or those lacking capacity. They might at best tell us what is best for the average child or person lacking capacity, but they do not tell us about the particular individual before the court. This is particularly true given the kind of cases which come before the court, which typically do not involve average people or average families. This was recognised by the Supreme Court in *Re B (a Child)* (2009) where the court urged judges to focus on an assessment of the welfare of the particular child in the context of the particular relationships he lived in, rather than on presumptions about welfare or arguments based on rights.

3.9 Criticisms of Relational Welfare

Relational understandings of well-being and welfare have been criticised. We look now at some of the concerns.

3.9.1 Lack of Protection

At the heart of many concerns is the fear that relational understandings might lead to reduced protection of the interests of children and incapacitous adults. Over recent years there have been many news stories about the abuse of adults in hospitals, care homes and community housing (e.g. Care Quality Commission 2012). Child abuse and mistreatment continue to dominate the headlines. History teaches us, as do current events, how easily those who cannot stand up for themselves can have their interests downtrodden by those with more power. Any theory that facilitates abuse or mistreatment is rightly treated with deep suspicion.

The best interests and welfare tests send important symbolic messages about children and incapacitous adults. These people must not be treated as second class citizens. They are least well placed socially and in the court setting, to represent their own interests, and hence it is vital that their interests are at the forefront of the judge's mind (James, James and McNamee 2003). Lucinda Ferguson (2013) has expressed concern that our views may deny the special position of children as deserving of particular attention and concern. We need, she insists, a detached view of children's interests, identified independently and not lumped together with their parents. Penney Lewis (2002) has written powerfully of the dangers of using people who lack capacity as a means to the end of others achieving "public good".

These concerns are well made: we support them. But let us be clear: we are not seeking to undermine the best interests or welfare principle. We entirely support the notion that children and those lacking capacity should have their interests made a priority in the eyes of the court. What we are discussing is how those interests are to be understood. We are arguing that their interests must be understood in the relational context and with an awareness *of* all the relevant responsibilities.

The objections assume that we could conceive of the interests of the child or incapacitous adult "in a detached way". But that, we suggest, is not only impossible, but dangerous. To look at the child outside the context of the relationships with their carers is highly artificial and would exclude much of what is of value to a child. The relationship-based formulation of the welfare principle is more realistic: it acknowledges the relationships within which the child is living and is likely to live; it looks at the 'gives and takes' of the past, present and future.

The dangers of not recognizing the relational approach for children or incapacitous adults are well demonstrated by *Re M* (*Child's Upbringing*) (1996). The Court of Appeal had to consider what should happen to a 10 year-old Zulu boy who had been handed over by his parents to a white couple and raised in England for 4 years. The child had settled into life in England and expressed a strong wish to stay with the white couple. There was expert evidence that his immediate return to South Africa would cause psychological harm. However, his parents successfully applied for his return, and Neill LJ stated:

> Of course there will be cases where the welfare of the child requires that the child's right to be with his natural parents has to give way in his own interest to other considerations. But I am satisfied that in this case, as in other cases, one starts with the strong supposition that it is in the [child's] best interests. … that he should be brought up with his natural parents.

The court therefore ordered the child to be returned immediately return to the natural parents. The story did not end there. After the court hearing, and some unsuccessful attempts to force him onto the aeroplane, the boy was returned to South Africa. But he failed to settle there and his family later consented to him being returned to the couple in England.

One can only imagine the trauma this child went through because the case was not dealt with in line with some of the principles outlined in this book. There was a failure to recognize the importance of the caring relationship that had developed between him and the foster carers. There was an inappropriate emphasis on the "relationship" with the birth family, even though at a day to day level it had no meaning for the child. The case highlights the dangers of using generalized presumptions rather than focussing on the particular issues faced by by a particular child. It indicates the importance of looking both to the past and the future, and of assessing the strength of the relationships which have built up over time. It stresses the need to look at the issue from the point of view of the child—namely that the most important people for him were those who loved him, day in day out.

Another example of the dangers of not considering the relational context and the importance of virtue is *Re Y* (*Mental Patient: Bone Marrow Donation*) (1997). A 25 year old woman (Y) lacked capacity and lived in a community home, where she was regularly visited by her mother. Y's sister suffered from a bone disorder. She could only recover if she found an appropriate bone marrow donor. The only suitable donor was Y. The sister sought a declaration that the harvesting of Y's bone marrow be authorised. Connell J granted the declaration. The donation would be in Y's best interests. The reasoning is revealing. It was explained that Y's mother was very important to Y's welfare. Y was anxious due to the sister's illness. If the sister died this would have a severe impact on the mother's health and this would, in turn, impact on Y's welfare. It was, therefore, in Y's welfare to donate the marrow. The physical discomfort and invasion caused by the donation were outweighed by the emotional and psychological benefits. This argument shows the dangers of the traditional best interests approach. The same reasoning could be used if Y's sister needed cosmetic surgery that would give the mother pleasure, and using tissue from Y would help the surgery go well. By the same reasoning, putting degrading photographs of Y on the internet could be justified if it gave the mother pleasure and improved her contact with Y. Under our approach the correct question would be whether, given the relations between Y, her mother and her sister, the giving of the bone marrow could be seen as a fair and virtuous part of the give and take of that relationship. Is it one of the reasonably required obligations, given the broad context of the relevant relationships? Does it require an excessive display of virtue? Hyper-altruism might be psychopathological, and enforcing altruism on incapacitous patients will in some circumstances be simply abusive. We suggest that it may well be that giving bone marrow would be acceptable, but taking photographs or donating material for cosmetic surgery would not. Our approach, therefore, offers more, not less, protection for the adult lacking capacity.

We do accept that it would be possible to misuse a relational approach to produce outcomes which would be harmful for the individual. However, that is true of any theory of wellbeing or welfare.

These two examples indicate that while opponents of our approach may claim that only a "detached view" of children's interests or the interests of adult lacking capacity, ensures their protection, in fact the "detached view" carries real dangers of its own. It creates an artificial view of the world, one which will not resonate with the child's perception of reality. The relational, virtue-based approach ensures that the interests of children and adults lacking capacity are placed centre stage, by recognizing what is of most value to children and adults lacking capacity.

3.9.2 Unpredictability

A different criticism of the relational, virtue based test we have suggested is that its application is unpredictable (Mnookin 1975). It can be difficult enough to predict what factors the courts will weigh up, let alone predict what the result will be. In *Re S (Adult Patient: Sterilisation)* (2001, p. 30) Thorpe LJ stated:

> in deciding what is best .... the judge must have regard to .... welfare as the paramount consideration. That embraces issues far wider than the medical. Indeed it would be undesirable and probably impossible to set bounds to what is relevant to a welfare determination.

We accept that the results of a relational, virtue based best interests or welfare test will be unpredictable. Indeed we rejoice in that. As we have already explained in this chapter, it is crucial that we do not rely on rules or presumptions that might make the results more predictable. Each case must be considered on its own merits, accepting the unique character and relational context of the person involved. Inevitably this produces a personalised result which is hard to predict: it is all the better for that.

3.9.3 *Can the Incapacitous Display Virtue?*

There is an obvious and strong objection to our view. Is it virtuous to have a virtuous decision made on your behalf? Does compelled altruism lose the moral virtue of altruism? Many people will take the view that a person cannot be virtuous or be said to have met their responsibilities, if they are compelled to do so by a court order. Only the autonomous, it might be said, can be virtuous. Children and those lacking capacity have no chance of being virtuous or meet their responsibilities. We disagree. We would question the assumption that choice is central to the notion of a virtue. There are two reasons.

First, virtues are not necessarily an expression of rational choice. Anyone relating to those lacking mental capacity knows that the incapacitous rarely lack the desires, attitudes, sensibilities or expectations that can form the basis of a virtue. In these attributes, and in their cultivation, virtue can be found. The toddler who cuddles the crying friend exhibits compassion and empathy, even if she lacks the mental capacity to express it in those terms. The love and care exhibited there is a simple expression of feeling. We should not confuse inability to articulate with inability to feel or express.

Second: our assumption that 'we' (the capacitous adults) have the autonomy and strength to be virtuous, while 'they' (children and those lacking capacity) do not, involves not only a misunderstanding of virtue, but also an inflated view of ourselves. We might like to pretend we are autonomous and strong (Herring 2012). The reality is a little less grand. The exhausted carer returning the demented adult to bed in the early hours of the morning may not be in the sort of rationally reflective way that we tend to associate with capacity, but is capacitous nonentheless. Many of our virtuous activities are not (at least primarily) a reflection of rational capacity. Indeed, the lover who loves without thinking, the hero who unthinkingly throws himself on the grenade to save his comrades, and the widow giving her mite without a second thought, all show remarkable virtue. Rationality has little to do with it. Indeed we might think slightly less of their acts if it did. We see the virtuous act as a supra-rational, unconscious expression of a desirable character. Calculation would dilute the virtue.

So, then, we reject arguments that only the autonomous can exercise virtue. Indeed, we wonder if anyone could make such a claim if they spent meaningful time with children or adults lacking capacity. Fortunately, the virtues of love, gentleness, kindness, wonder are open to all, whether trained in rational thought or not.

3.10 Conclusion

This chapter sought to outline how the more theoretical ideas in Chaps. 2–4 could be put into a concrete legal concept of best interests or welfare. Our idea about how 'welfare' and 'best interests' should be approached is, we accept, open to the charge of vagueness. It has no "rules" and little predictability. But that is precisely the point. It emphasises the importance of understanding the particular unique child in the particular circumstances that he or she is in and the relationships within which the child or incapacitous adult lives. Only by appreciating the significance of these and the responsibilities and rights that flow from them can be we begin to fashion a result which might work within that context and determine which court order will promote the individual's welfare or best interests. Inevitably this will be a heavily context- dependent assessment: it cannot be codified in a set of rules or axioms. We have, however, tried to indicate some of the issues that a responsible judge will take into account.

We emphasised that we are seeking to enable children and adults lacking capacity to flourish in the context of good relationships. Good relationships entail give and take, and responsibilities as well as rights. They promote autonomy, but not in a way which means that the person whose autonomy is promoted will be able to take every decision as they wish. Life is not like that. By emphasising the importance of needs, respect, responsibility and relationality, we sought to indicate what a good caring relationship looks like.

We also showed that the importance of relationships in identifying and sustaining the self requires the courts to take abuse within intimate relationships particularly seriously. Just as relationships can build up a person to be the best they can be, they can knock a person down the lowest pit. We explained that a relational approach requires that questions about welfare/best interests be seen in the context of the relationship between the parties, and that that involves looking back at how the relationship has developed to date and how it is likely to develop in the future.

Finally we defended our claims against critics. We rejected the suggestion that our approach fails to protect children or prioritise their interests. Quite the opposite: it understands those interests in a rich and full way. We also rejected concerns that our approach is unpredictable, because its appeal lies in unpredictability, or at least necessitates unpredictability, since it advocates an approach fashioned to meet the needs of the particular child or adult lacking capacity. We also confronted and rejected the claim that only the autonomous can show virtue. Rather, we argued that we if had eyes to see, the virtue of children and adults lacking capacity would be all too apparent: the law can help to give us those eyes, and it certainly needs such eyes itself.

References

Arnault L (2003) Cruelty, horror, and the will to redemption. Hypatia 18:155–183
Archard D (2001) Philosophical perspectives on childhood. In: Fionda J (ed) Legal concepts of childhood. Hart, Oxford, pp 52–75
Bridgeman J (2009) Parental responsibility, young children and healthcare law. Cambridge University Press, Cambridge
Care Quality Commission (2012) Our market report. Care Quality Commission, London
Carle S (2005) Theorizing agency. Am. Univ Law Rev 55:307–365
Clark Miller S (2005) Need, care and obligation. R Inst Philos Suppl 57:157–173
Clement G (1996) Care, autonomy and justice: feminism and the ethic of care. Westview, Boulder
Curk P (2011) Passions, dependencies, selves. In: Lind C, Keating H, Bridgeman J (eds) Taking responsibility, law and the changing family. Ashgate, Aldershot, pp 51–67
Czapanskiy K (1999) Interdependency, caretakers and children. Santa Clara Law Rev 39:957–1089
Dalmiya V (2002) Why should a knower care? Hypatia 17:34–56
Dillon R (1992) Respect and care. Can J Philos 22:105–134
Dodds S (2005) Gender, ageing, and injustice: social and political contexts of bioethics. J Med Ethics 31(5):295–298
Dodds S (2007) Depending on care: recognition of vulnerability and the social contribution of care provision. Bioethics 21:500–531
Eekelaar J (1994) The interests of the child and the child's wishes. The role of dynamic self-determinism. Int J Law Policy Fam 8:42–66
Eekelaar J (2006) Family law and personal life. Oxford University Press, Oxford
England K, Dyck I (2011) Managing the body work of home care. Sociol Health Illn 33:206–233
Engster D (2007) The heart of justice. Care ethics and political theory. Oxford University Press, Oxford
Fink J (2004) Care personal lives and social policy. Policy Press, Bristol
Ferguson L (2013) Not merely rights for children but children's rights: the theory gap and the assumption of the importance of children's rights. Int J Child Rights 21:177–212
Gilligan C (1982) In a different voice. Harvard University Press, Cambridge
Groenhout R (2004) Connected lives: human nature and an ethics of care. Rowman and Littlefield, New York
Held V (2006) The ethics of care. Oxford University Press, Oxford
Herring J (2011) No more having and holding: the abolition of the marital rape exemption. In: Gilmore S, Herring J, Probert R (eds) Landmarks in family law. Hart, Oxford
Herring J (2012) Vulnerability, children and the law. In: Freeman M (ed) Law and childhood studies. Oxford University Press, Oxford
Herring J (2013) Caring and the law. Hart, Oxford
Herring J (2014a) The disability critique of care. Elder Law Rev 8:1–19
Herring J (2014b) The welfare principle and the children act: presumably it's about welfare? J Soc Welf Fam Law 36:14–31
Herring J, Wall J (2014) Understanding capacity: the heart may easily overrule the head. Elder Law J 4:190–201
Itzen C, Taket A, Barter-Godfrey S (2010) Domestic and sexual violence and abuse. Routledge, Abingdon
James A, James A, McNamee S (2003) Constructing children's welfare in family proceedings. Family Law 33:889–893
Khodyakov D (2007) Trust as a process: a three dimensional approach. Sociology 41:116–133
Leckey R (2007) Contracting claims and family law feuds. Univ Tor Law J 57:1–41
Lewis P (2002) Procedures that are against the medical interests of the incompetent person. Oxf J Leg Stud 12:575–601

Mnookin R (1975) Child-custody adjudication: judicial functions in the face of indeterminacy. Law Contemp Probl 39:259–312

Munby LJ (2010) Consent to treatment. In: Grubb A, Laing J, McHale J (eds) Principles of medical law. Oxford University Press, Oxford, p 548

Noddings N (1984) Caring: a feminine approach to ethics and moral education. University of California Press, Berkeley

Rachmilovitz O (2007) Bringing down the bedroom walls: emphasizing substance over form in personalized abuse. William Mary J Women Law 14:495–541

Sevenhuijsen S (2003) The place of care: the relevance of the feminist ethic of care for social policy. Feminist Theor 4:179–201

Sevenhuijsen S (1998) Citizenship and the ethics of care. Routledge, Abingdon

Shakespeare T (2000) Help venture. London

Stark E (2007) Coercive control. Oxford University Press, Oxford

Tietjens Meyers D (2004) Narrative and moral life. In: Calhoun C (ed) Setting the moral compass. Oxford University Press, Oxford

Tronto J (1983) Moral boundaries: a political argument for an ethic of care. Routledge, Abingdon

Ungerson C (ed) (1990) Gender and caring: work and welfare in Britain and Scandinavia. Harvester Wheatsheaf, London

Wiles J (2011) Reflections on being a recipient of care: vexing the concept of vulnerability. Soc Cult Geogr 12:573

Williams F (2002) The presence of feminism in the future of welfare. Econ Soc 31:502–533

Woodhouse B (1993) Hatching the egg: a child-centered perspective on parents' rights. Cardozo Law Rev 14:1747–1821

Chapter 4
What Do the Courts Do?

Abstract This chapter explores how the courts have applied the welfare test or best interests principles. We argue that although the courts are not normally explicit about doing so, they do in fact take into account the relational context of the case and the importance of promoting virtue. We suggest, therefore, that the understanding of welfare and best interests promoted in this book would not entail a significant change either to the outcome of most cases or to the substance of the reasoning, but we contend that it would be more satisfactory if the courts acknowledged explicitly their use of relationality and virtue.

Keywords Welfare principle · Best interests · Sterilisation · Bone marrow · Medical research

4.1 Introduction

To summarise the points made in this book so far: we have argued that, properly understood, the notions of well-being and best interests include relationality, altruism and virtue. Therefore in assessing welfare or best interests it is crucial that the individual is considered within the context of the relationships within which they live, and that the importance of those relationships as an essential substrate of their welfare is acknowledged, together with the obligations that flow from the relationships. In the previous chapter we indicated how a court might understand the notions of best interests and welfare. In this chapter we suggest that our proposals are not utterly revolutionary: they are consonant with the way the courts have in fact understood welfare and best interests. In other words we seek to argue that our explanation of best interests and welfare makes explicit what the courts *are* doing, rather than demanding a radical rethinking of the concepts.

First it is necessary to set out the statutory framework.

C. Foster and J. Herring, *Altruism, Welfare and the Law*,
SpringerBriefs in Law, DOI 10.1007/978-3-319-21605-8_4

4.2 The Statutory Framework

The Children Act 1989 opens (Section 1) with one of the central principles of English family law[1]:

When a court determines any question with respect to—

(a) the upbringing of a child; or
(b) the administration of a child's property or the application of any income arising from it the child's welfare shall be the court's paramount consideration.

Section 1(3) provides a checklist of factors a judge should consider when assessing the welfare of the child:

(a) the ascertainable wishes and feelings of the child concerned (considered in the light of his age and understanding);
(b) his physical, emotional and educational needs;
(c) the likely effect on him of any change in his circumstances;
(d) his age, sex, background and any characteristics of his which the court considers relevant;
(e) any harm which he has suffered or is at risk of suffering;
(f) how capable each of his parents, and any other person in relation to whom the court considers the question to be relevant, is of meeting his needs;
(g) the range of powers available to the court under this Act in the proceedings in question.

Under the Mental Capacity Act 2005, if a person lacks capacity a decision maker can make decisions on their behalf. The Act provides in Section 1(5) that:

An act done, or decision made, under this Act for or on behalf of a person who lacks capacity must be done, or made, in his best interests.

Section 4(6) lists some of the key factors to be taken into account—

(a) the person's past and present wishes and feelings (and, in particular, any relevant written statement made by him when he had capacity),
(b) the beliefs and values that would be likely to influence his decision if he had capacity, and
(c) the other factors that he would be likely to consider if he were able to do so.

The Department of Constitutional Affairs (2007, para 5.7) *Mental Capacity Act: Code of Practice* states:

> When working out what is in the best interests of the person who lacks capacity to make a decision or act for themselves, decision-makers must take into account all relevant factors that it would be reasonable to consider, not just those that they think are important. They must not act or make a decision based on what they would want to do if they were the person who lacked capacity.

[1]A detailed analysis of the welfare principle and its interpretation can be found in Herring (2015: Chap 10).

4.3 The Interpretation of the Welfare and Best Interests Tests

There has been considerable debate over the meaning of the word 'paramount' in Section 1(1) of the Children Act 1989. The accepted interpretation is that it means that the welfare of child is the sole consideration,[2] and that accordingly the interests of adults and other children are only relevant in so far as they impact on the welfare of the child.[3]

The court typically follows the course of action which it sees as best promoting the interests of the child, viewed as an atomistic entity, regardless of the impact such an order will have on the interests of the child's parents, any other children or the wider community. As was stated by the Court of Appeal in *Re P (Contact: Supervision)* (1996, 328), 'the court is concerned with the interests of the mother and the father only in so far as they bear on the welfare of the child'. A good illustration is *Re C (A Child)* (2012) where a father had been imprisoned after abusing his child (C). The first instance judge had ordered that he could not have contact with C, but that he should be sent a passport size photograph of C every year. The Court of Appeal overturned the order. Although the photograph would provide comfort to C, in no way did it promote C's welfare. The order could not be justified based on the benefit to the father. This is true even in the case of "unimpeachable" (perfect) parents, as was made clear in *J* v *C* (1970).

Similarly, the best interests test in the Mental Capacity Act 2005 appears to focus on the best interests of the person lacking capacity ('P'). It is true that family members and those involved in P's care can be consulted, but the decision-maker is to take into account only their views on what is best for P (Pattinson 2011, p. 147). Their interests in their own right are not relevant factors (Mental Capacity Act 2005, Section 4; Manthorpe et al. 2007). Lord Brandon in *F v West Berkshire HA* (1989, p. 551) stated:

> The operation or other treatment will be in their best interests if, but only if, it is carried out in order either to save their lives or to ensure improvement or prevent deterioration in their physical or mental health.

So: under the Mental Capacity Act and the Children Act, the position seems at first sight to be that it is only permissible to take into account the impact on third parties in so far as it impacts on P. If a decision will harm the carer of the child or of P's carer, and that means that they would no longer be able to care for the child or

[2]UN Convention on the Rights of Children, in Article 3, states that the child's welfare should be the primary consideration. This appears to place slightly less weight on children's interests than s 1 of the Children Act 1989.

[3]Lord Hobhouse in *Dawson v Wearmouth* [1999] 1 FLR 1167. Although see Herring (1999a, b) for an argument that despite this the courts have in fact found means of giving weight to parents and other children.

P, then that can be taken into account (*NHS Trust v DE* (2013); *Re Y* (*mental incapacity: bone marrow transplant*) (1997) and *Re A* (*Male Sterilisation*) (2000)). Otherwise it cannot. Such an interpretation might appear to require the court to make an order which would very slightly improve the welfare of the child or incapacitous adult even though that would cause a huge level of harm to others. However, in practice, as we shall see shortly, the court has found a variety of ways of avoiding these conclusions. The cases reveal that, unsurprisingly, both the interests of the individual's family members and carers, and what is reasonably virtuous, are factors to be taken into account. This creates a difficulty. The courts do not seem to be giving effect to the principle they purport to follow. In Chap. 3 we presented an understanding of welfare and best interests which makes it entirely appropriate to take into account the interests of others and the demands of virtue when making welfare or best interests assessments. We believe, therefore, that the courts could and should stand by the welfare and best interests principle, while still taking account of the welfare of others enmeshed in the nexus of caring relationships in which P exists.

We will now explore the interpretation of, first, the best interests test under the Mental Capacity Act, and then the welfare principle under the Children Act. Properly read, we suggest, these reflect two themes that run through our understanding of welfare and best interests. The first is that the welfare of people is tied up with their relationships. We cannot consider the interests of P without thinking about the interests of those with whom they are in relationship. And second: that acting in a reasonably virtuous or altruistic way can and should be seen as acting a person's best interests. Both these claims are supported by the authorities.

4.4 The Importance of the Relational Context in Mental Capacity Act Cases

In *Re MM* (2007, para 99) Munby J (as he then was) summarized well the approach that should be adopted in determining a person's best interests:

> MM's welfare is the paramount consideration. The focus must be on MM's best interests, and this involves a welfare appraisal in the widest sense, taking into account, where appropriate, a wide range of ethical, social, moral, emotional and welfare considerations. Where, as will often be the case, the various factors engaged pull in opposite directions, the task of ascertaining where the individual's best interests truly lie will be assisted by preparation of a 'balance sheet' of the kind suggested by Thorpe LJ in *Re A (Male Sterilisation)* [2000] 1 FLR 549 at p. 560. This will enable the judge, at the end of the day, to strike what Thorpe LJ referred to as 'a balance between the sum of the certain and possible gains against the sum of the certain and possible losses.'

How have the courts used this approach? We are not offering, of course, a complete analysis of the case law. Rather we select cases where the issues concerning relationality and virtue are particularly apparent.

4.4.1 *Great Western NHS Trust v AA [2014] EWHC 132 (Fam)*

In this case AA was 25, pregnant and had bipolar disorder. She had been compliant with the antenatal care offered to her, but towards the later part of her pregnancy had stopped taking medication. Her medical team determined that due to complications with her pregnancy, a Caesarean Section was needed. She refused to consent, but it was found that she lacked capacity to refuse. A best interests assessment was required. In declaring that the best interests assessment justified the operation, Hayden J was clear that it had to focus on AA and not on the interests of the fetus:

> I have addressed here the disadvantages to the mother in this process conducting a balance of the positives and negatives in the competing alternatives. I do so because I am not in this application concerned with the welfare of the foetus It must be said however that the alternative to the elective cesarean plainly carries significant risks to the foetus or to the baby and the real clinical prospect of foetal distress.

However, he went on to explain:

> When I consider the best interests of AA here, I do so by evaluating the clinical alternatives keeping her medical interests in focus. But a best interests decision requires a broader survey of the available material. I am perfectly satisfied that this is a wanted baby in a supportive family unit. I have listened carefully to what the family has said, particularly what AA's partner, BB, has said. … I believe that he was telling me that if AA were not florid, if she were not suffering this profound psychotic episode, and if she were in a position to reason her situation objectively, she would follow the recommendation of the doctors.

The judge clearly accepted the idea that the views of family members as to what AA would want if she had capacity could be taken into account. That is uncontroversial: an element of substituted judgment has plainly been imported into the Act by virtue of s. 4(6) and 4(7). However, he went further than that, recognising the "supportive family unit" and the father's attitude towards the family as being significant factors in an assessment of well-being. Had the husband strongly opposed the proposed procedure or been unkeen on caring for the child, the assessment might have been different. The husband's views and attitudes could not be separated from determining what was best for AA.

4.4.2 *Ahsan v Universities Hospital Leicester [2006] EWHC 2624 (QB)*

This important case emphasised the importance of respecting the values of a community that a person has lived within.[4] Mrs. Ahsan had been severely injured in

[4]Similar endorsement of the views of the community can be derived from cases permitting (for instance), male circumcision.

an accident and was "wholly unaware of her surroundings". The issue arose as to whether she should be cared for at home (and therefore in compliance with her Muslim beliefs), or cared for in a hospital. It was argued that as she lacked capacity "any familial, social, cultural, religious or spiritual considerations" could be ignored. The issue was summarised in this way:

> The point arises so starkly because Mrs. Ahsan's immediate family are devout Muslims. They firmly believe that she should be cared for at home in a Muslim environment where they could pray together in her presence and ensure the proper observance of Muslim traditions and practices. The simple argument advanced on behalf of the Defendant is that Mrs. Ahsan is and will continue to be wholly unaware of any of these matters and that she can therefore derive no provable benefit from it (para 43).

The defendant's argument was fiercely rejected by Judge Hegarty QC:

> But I do not agree. I do not think for one moment that a reasonable member of the public would consider that the religious beliefs of an individual and her family should simply be disregarded in deciding how she should be cared for in the unhappy event of supervening mental incapacity. On the contrary, I would have thought that most reasonable people would expect, in the event of some catastrophe of that kind, that they would be cared for, as far as practicable, in such a way as to ensure that they were treated with due regard for their personal dignity and with proper respect for their religious beliefs (para 51).

The significance of this decision is that is that it recognises the importance of the fact that for Ms. Ahsan her membership of the Muslim community was central to her identity as a person. A person who loses capacity does not cease being a member of their family or community. For Mrs. Ahsan her wellbeing could not be separated from her position as a Muslim.

4.4.3 A Local Authority v A and B [2010] EWHC 978 (Fam)

This decision involved two families caring for people with Magenis Syndrome, a rare genetic disorder that has physical, medical and neuropsychiatric manifestations. The issue raised was whether it was permissible for the family to lock the child or adult into their rooms at night. The families had done this so that they would not cause themselves serious harm. The alternative of constant supervision would mean that the carers would get no sleep. The legal issue turned on whether the locking in the room amounted to a deprivation of liberty. The conclusion on this is revealing:

> In neither home does the regime involve a deprivation of liberty. And in saying this I should make clear that I do not see this as being a borderline case or a case which falls to be decided on a fine balance. In my judgment, the loving, caring, regime in each of these family homes – a reasonable, proportionate and entirely appropriate regime implemented by devoted parents in the context of a loving family relationship and with the single view to the welfare, happiness and best interests of A and C respectively – falls significantly short of anything that would engage Article 5 (para 115).

What is striking about this analysis is that it sidelines any legal analysis of the nature of a deprivation of liberty. Instead the focus is on the nature of the relationship. A loving relationship would aim to promote the welfare and happiness of the individuals. A narrow construction might have concluded that being locked in their room at night was against the patients' best interests, and consequently an unjustified deprivation of liberty. However, looked at broadly and relationally, it could be seen as arising out of the patient's network of loving relationships, and hence promoting their welfare (Dunn and Herring 2011).

4.4.4 *A Local Authority v WMA [2013] EWCOP 2580 (Fam)*

This case considered whether a young man should be removed from his mother and placed in an independent setting. The young man was clear that he wished to remain living with his mother. The mother wanted him to remain too. The judge, however, decided that the son should move. He properly looked not just at the *fact* of the relationship but at whether it was marked by care and respect. He concluded:

> It is difficult to determine his personal wishes because I have concluded that whatever they may be they are dominated by MA to such a degree that he is probably mouthing her words. For all that, I have to be very careful as to the weight to be attached to his wishes and feelings.

There were serious concerns over the care given by the mother, of whom the judge commented, tactfully:

> The sad truth is she has huge limitations as a carer for WMA. She has poor eyesight, she cannot budget, she cannot keep food hygienically, she cannot keep the home clean and tidy, rather the reverse. She is opposed to regular engagement with local authority professionals. She will not work with the local authority on her own admission and she has spurned help from Delos herself. Whatever she may say about being a good mother to WMA, and I am sure she intends to be one, she is, in practice, a poor one; for she has done little to forward his learning social and self care skills.

What we see here is the court interrogating the nature of the relationship between WMA and his mother. Note the careful attention to the details of the relationship and the quality of the care. While we might argue about the outcome, the judgement is marked by its attention to the history and prospective aspects of the relationship. Notably the court wanted the relationship between mother and son to continue:

> I accept, of course, the local authority must continue to respect private and family life for WMA. He must continue to see MA for regular contact and his best interests must not be prejudiced; yet it is clear his private life will be enhanced by moving. Indeed, the relationship with MA might even improve because there will be an end to that worrying mutuality referred to by Dr. Carpenter. I appreciate that the move may be an interference in MA's private life and family life but it is more than justified in the circumstances.

The judgement reveals a close analysis of the relational context and an attempt to provide a solution which could enable WMA to flourish within caring relationships.

4.4.5 *NHS Trust v DE [2013] EWHC 2562 (Fam)*

In this case it was determined that DE, an adult who lacked capacity, should have a vasectomy. The difficulty was that it was hard to see how a vasectomy would directly benefit DE. As Butler Sloss LJ had stated in *Re A* (*Male Sterilisation*) (2000, p. 557)

> The sterilisation of a man is not the equivalent of an application in respect of a woman. .. sexual intercourse for a woman carries the risk of pregnancy. .. there is no direct consequence for a man of sexual intercourse other than the possibility of sexually transmitted diseases.

DE's vasectomy was justified on a number of bases. First, a strong preference for the vasectomy had been voiced by DE's parents, his primary carers, as it would reduce the worry that he might father a child. Their concerns could be taken into account because:

> DE is very close to his parents; he loves and relies upon them. If they are upset he is upset. The court can take into account the benefits to FG and JK of DE having a vasectomy if it is a factor DE would consider if he had capacity. It is likely that DE would consider the benefit to his parents of relieving them of the anxiety and strain that they have been suffering and of which he has been very conscious.

Second, if the vasectomy took place, the relationship between DE and PQ, a woman with whom he had a close relationship, could continue unsupervised. Without the vasectomy, concerns about pregnancy meant their time together had to be restricted and supervised.

> Such a benefit to the parents would be of significant benefit to DE, not only because he would benefit from them being happier and less anxious, but also because relieved of the anxiety of a second pregnancy, I am satisfied that JK would feel able significantly to relax the level of supervision she felt to be necessary and that, despite her general misgivings about PQ, would once again promote and support the relationship as she did prior to the pregnancy.
>
> DE's relationship with PQ is enduring and loving. It is very important to DE and he was deeply distressed when there was a break at the beginning of the year. The relationship should be respected and supported in the way all other aspects of DE's life are respected and supported.

In this case the importance of the relationship between DE and PQ to DE's welfare was emphasised and given considerable weight. It was acknowledged that relationship carried with it responsibilities—such as DE's responsibility to avoid getting his partner pregnant.

4.4.6 *A LA v JH [2011] EWHC 2420 (COP)*

Here, Mrs. H's medical/social care team wished to move her from her husband so that she could be better cared for in a nursing home. At the heart of the judicial rejection of that proposal was that moving Mrs. H would mean separating her from the most important person in her life. It is notable that the medical/social care team had treated Mrs. H's well-being as being concerned purely with her physical body, and were particularly influenced by how well her husband could use items of equipment designed to help that body. It was right that judge emphasised the relational values that were in fact key to her well-being. DJ Eldergill explained:

> The quality of Mrs. H's relationship with her husband, the strength of their marriage, and the fundamental importance of that relationship to her happiness and indeed her care, have deserved considerable weight.

Quite correctly he thought the case could be put no better than Mr. H had put it before the court. Mr. H's statement about the significance of relational values to people is worth quoting in full:

> What I will say is that I have been married to JH for over thirty years and during that time we have been devoted to one another. I do not consider it to be an understatement to say that we cannot live without each other and if the court went against my wife, mine and the wishes of her family and placed her in a nursing home I believe it would be the end of us. I do not say this lightly and I do not want this to be interpreted as a threat, it is a simple fact.
>
> One thing I would wish to make clear is that this is our life, [JH] and mine, we have lived together happily for over thirty years and are still devoted to one another. The professionals involved have come into our lives and instead of trying to understand us they have tried to impose their thoughts about JH's care on us. These people will come and go, there will be different carers, social workers and district nurses that will come and go from our lives, but we are each others constants. We are husband and wife and this is our life, this is not work, not something we will be involved in for a few months here and there before we move onto a new client but it is our life and the outcome of theses proceedings have the ability to break up a loving family because we are considered to be difficult. I am made out to be causing harm to my wife, this is simply not true. The care I provide to my wife stems from the love and respect I have for her and the wish for her to be happy. The care I give her is not because I am being paid to do it. When I give her care I am not restrained in the time I can dedicate to her because I have several other service users that need my attention as would be the case if she were placed in a nursing home. The level of care I can provide for my wife will always be superior to that provided by people employed to provide it.
>
> It can be seen that from the evidence of the local authority there has been no reference to any criticism of the care I have provided to her.
> I know that I may come across as being difficult and that I may appear to be a stubborn man, but everything I have ever done has always been with the belief that I am doing in her best interests.

4.4.7 Statutory Provisions About Medical Research

Sections 30–34 of the Mental Capacity Act 2005 allow medical research to be conducted on subjects lacking capacity. The subject in such a research situation will probably never meet most of the beneficiaries. Indeed P may die before the study is completed. It may seem that, in the realm of research, the best interests test is abandoned. The traditional, atomistic understanding of best interests would have difficulty in endorsing research on P that could only benefit others. That, we suggest, is because that traditional understanding is wrong. The endorsement of this kind of research does not mark a radical departure from the fundamental principle that clinical (or any other) interference with P, if it is in P's best interests. This is better seen as an example of P's best interests being construed in the light of a realization that the interests of one are ultimately continuous with those of others. We return to the question of research on subjects lacking capacity in Chap. 5, where we suggest that the World Medical Association's Declaration of Helsinki—the most authoritative set of guidelines on research on human subjects—endorses our approach.

4.5 The Importance of Altruism and Virtue in Mental Capacity Act Cases

We move now to cases where the courts have acknowledged the importance of altruism and virtue as constituent parts of a person's welfare or best interests.

4.5.1 Re X, Y and Z [2014] EWHC 87 (COP)

In this case a mother had been seriously injured in a car accident and had been awarded a substantial sum of damages. Her injuries meant that she lacked capacity to make decisions for herself. The question arose whether some of her damages should be used to pay for a nanny and for other expenses incurred in bringing up her children. The case was made difficult by the fact that payments to the children would reduce the sums that could be paid for the mother's own care. For the future care of the children, some £165,000 would be needed over the course of 6 years. Nevertheless it was held that the payments made for the children's care could be regarded as being made in the best interests of the mothers.

In part this best interests assessment relied on the fact that while the mother had had capacity it was clear she wanted to support her children. However, and more interestingly, it was also justified in these terms:

> Where a parent loses mental capacity at a time when she is still responsible for her children, those responsibilities are part of her "interests" which have to be addressed by those making

> decisions on her behalf, and payments to meet the reasonable needs of those children are manifestly capable of being described as in her "best interests".

This is a welcome acknowledgement that (onerous) fulfilment of a person's responsibilities can be seen as part of their best interests.

4.5.2 RE G(T) [2010] EWHC 3005 (Fam)

In *Re G (TJ)* (2010) a woman had lost capacity. The question arose whether payments she had been making to her adult daughter, of whom she was fond and who was in financial need, should continue. Morgan J held that:

> the word "interests" in the phrase "best interests" is not confined to matters of self interest or, putting it another way, a court could conclude in an appropriate case that it is in the interests of P for P to act altruistically. It seems unlikely that the legislature thought that the power to make gifts should be confined to gifts which were not altruistic or where the gift would confer a benefit on P (or the donor of the lasting power of attorney) by reason of that person's emotional response to knowing of the gift.

Further,

> [T]he word 'interest' in the best interests test does not confine the court to considering the self-interest of P. The actual wishes of P, which are altruistic and not in any way, directly or indirectly self-interested, can be a relevant factor. Further, the wishes which P would have formed, if P had capacity, which may be altruistic wishes, can be a relevant factor (para 56).

As this case demonstrates, 'best interests' need not be interpreted in a narrow, selfish way. It can include acting altruistically to ones friends and family. This is not limited to cases where a person got on well with a family member, but applies when there would be a moral obligation towards them.

4.5.3 LG v DK [2011] EWHC 2453 (COP)

DK was aged 84 and had advanced dementia. He was unable to manage his own affairs. A solicitor, in acting for him, uncovered evidence that he may have a daughter. BJ, the putative daughter, sought use of a bodily sample from DK to test whether or not she was indeed the daughter. The proceedings were brought by the Official Aolicitor and not BJ. It was made clear in the judgement that BH was not "motivated by mercenary considerations". There had only been very limited contact between DK and BJ previously. BJ's only wish was to have contact with DK and maintain a father/daughter relationship. While the judgment is primarily about jurisdictional issues, and no final ruling was made about best interests, there was a strong indication that, despite some evidence of reluctance from DK to give a DNA sample previously "it would.....require unusual facts for DK's best interests to depart from the ascertainment of the truth or the interests of justice" (para 55). The court was acknowledging that playing one's part as a citizen to promote justice and truth within one's community can be regarded as promoting your best interests, even if you lack an appreciation that that is what you are doing.

4.5.4 The Mental Capacity Act Code of Practice

The Mental Capacity Act Code (Department for Constitutional Affairs 2007) seems open to the possibility that it might be in P's interests to behave altruistically. It gives the following example:

> Anita, a young woman, suffers serious brain damage during a car accident. The court appoints her father as deputy to invest the compensation she received. As the decision-maker he must think about her wishes, beliefs and values before deciding how to invest the money. Anita had worked for an overseas charity. Her father talks to her former colleagues. They tell him how Anita's political beliefs shaped her work and personal beliefs, so he decides not to invest in the bonds that a financial adviser had recommended, because they are from companies Anita would not have approved of. Instead, he employs an ethical investment adviser to choose appropriate companies in line with her beliefs.
>
> The Act allows actions that benefit other people, as long as they are in the best interests of the person who lacks capacity to make the decision. For example, having considered all the circumstances of the particular case, a decision might be made to take a blood sample from a person who lacks capacity to consent, to check for a genetic link to cancer within the family, because this might benefit someone else in the family. But it might still be in the best interests of the person who lacks capacity. 'Best interests' goes beyond the person's medical interests.
>
> For example, courts have previously ruled that possible wider benefits to a person who lacks capacity to consent, such as providing or gaining emotional support from close relationships, are important factors in working out the person's own best interests. If it is likely that the person who lacks capacity would have considered these factors themselves, they can be seen as part of the person's best interests.

4.6 The Welfare Principle in Family Law

Some of the arguments in this book have received explicit approval from the Court of Appeal in the case of *Re G* (*Education: Religious Upbringing*) (2011). The case involved a dispute between parents who had raised their five children, aged between 3 and 11, within the Chasidic (or Chareidi) community of ultra-orthodox Jews. When the marriage broke down the children resided with their mother, although they had extensive contact with the father. By this point the mother had left the Chareidi community, although she still considered herself an Orthodox Jew. The children attended a single sex ultra-orthodox school attended by other Chareidi community children. The main issue for the court concerned with whom the children should live and what schooling was most appropriate.

Munby LJ decided that the children should live with the mother, and should have contact with the father. He made some wide-ranging comments on the nature of children's welfare. We will focus on these. He emphasized that 'welfare' in Section 1 of the Children Act 1989 should be understood broadly to cover the child's well-being:

> Evaluating a child's best interests involves a welfare appraisal in the widest sense, taking into account, where appropriate, a wide range of ethical, social, moral, religious, cultural emotional and welfare considerations. Everything that conduces to a child's welfare and happiness or relates to the child's development and present and future life as a human being, including the child's familial, educational and social environment, and the child's social, cultural, ethnic and religious community, is potentially relevant and has, where appropriate, to be taken into account. The judge must adopt a holistic approach (para 27).

Referring to some of our earlier work (Herring and Foster 2012) he made it clear that welfare is not to be seen as a matter of happiness:

> I have referred to the child's happiness. Very recently, Herring and Foster... have argued persuasively that behind a judicial determinations of welfare there lies an essentially Aristotelian notion of the 'good life'. What then constitutes a 'good life'? There is no need to pursue here that age-old question. I merely emphasise that happiness, in the sense in which I have used the word, is not pure hedonism. It can include such things as the cultivation of virtues and the achievement of worthwhile goals, and all the other aims which parents routinely seek to inculcate in their children.

Munby LJ also emphasised the importance of relational values:

> The well-being of a child cannot be assessed in isolation. Human beings live within a network of relationships. Men and women are sociable beings. As John Donne famously remarked, "No man is an Island ..." Blackstone observed that "Man was formed for society". And long ago Aristotle said that "He who is unable to live in society, or who has no need because he is sufficient for himself, must be either a beast or a god". As Herring and Foster comment, relationships are central to our sense and understanding of ourselves. Our characters and understandings of ourselves from the earliest days are charted by reference to our relationships with others. It is only by considering the child's network of relationships that their well-being can be properly considered. So a child's relationships, both within and without the family, are always relevant to the child's interests; often they will be determinative (para 30).

Giving some further practical guidance, Munby LJ emphasised the need to act as a "judicial reasonable parent" and have regard to the general standards in (then) 2012 and the "ever-changing nature of the world". He expounded three aspects of this:

> First, we must recognise that equality of opportunity is a fundamental value of our society: equality as between different communities, social groupings and creeds, and equality as between men and women, boys and girls. Second, we foster, encourage and facilitate aspiration: both aspiration as a virtue in itself and, to the extent that it is practical and reasonable, the child's own aspirations. Far too many lives in our community are blighted, even today, by lack of aspiration. Third, our objective must be to bring the child to adulthood in such a way that the child is best equipped both to decide what kind of life they want to lead—what kind of person they want to be—and to give effect so far as practicable to their aspirations. Put shortly, our objective must be to maximise the child's opportunities

> in every sphere of life as they enter adulthood. And the corollary of this, where the decision has been devolved to a 'judicial parent', is that the judge must be cautious about approving a regime which may have the effect of foreclosing or unduly limiting the child's ability to make such decisions in future (para 80).

Applying these principles to the case, he ruled that the children should not be brought up in the Chareidi school, which discouraged children from pursuing further education and limited opportunities later in life, especially for girls. In saying that, he emphasised that the courts were neutral as between religions.

This case, both in its reasoning and outcome, echoes many of the arguments of this book. Children's welfare is not simply a matter of making them happy. Being raised in a community which treasures both boys and girls and discourages neither from fulfilling their dreams is an important aspect of welfare. Further the Court of Appeal emphasized that the network of the relationships was central to a child's well-being. One of the issues in relation to education which could have been raised is that, had the father won the argument over education, the children would be raised in a school which would have been critical of the way of the life they had with the mother. As Tamara Tolley (2014) suggests, had the children lived with the mother and it was she who wanted the children to go to the ultra-orthodox school, the dispute over education might have been decided differently.

Apart from the explicit acknowledgment of the relational and virtue values which are central to children's welfare in *Re G* and the law on medical research and children, we suggest that the whole architecture of family law is designed to protect family relationships generally (Herring 1999a, b). Note, for instance, that the law does not enforce minute by minute, day by day promotion by parents of their children's welfare. There is no active regulation of parenting or inspection of parental care in the way there is for day-care centres or child-minders (Children Act 1989, Part X, Sch 9). As a neighbour you may have strong views about the way the children next door are fed, clothed or education, but no court will hear your complaint, or even the complaint of a social worker, unless the harm amounts to significant harm and care proceedings are appropriate (Children Act 1989, s. 31). This, we suggest, denotes an overarching philosophy, not just an acknowledgement that the assumption of the burden of regulation would be administratively crushing or politically offensive. Note too that there are plenty of areas of family law where the welfare principle does not apply. In deciding whether or not to grant a divorce, for example, the claims for children count for nothing. In domestic violence and financial order cases, although the interests of children may be relevant, they are not treated as a paramount concern. This indicates that in relation to orders of particular significance for the intimate lives of the parents, consideration of the interests of the children can be subsumed into a consideration of the overall effect of a decision on the network of relationships in which both the parents and the children (and others) exist. This acknowledges that there are limits on the burdens that parents can be expected to bear in order to promote their children's welfare. Parents cannot be required to remain married, for instance, simply because it would make the children happy.

4.7 Conclusion

We admit that at first sight the welfare principle and the best interests test set out in the Children Act 1989 and the Mental Capacity Act 2005 respectively do not appear open to some of the arguments advanced in the book. That initial reaction is reinforced by some of the general statements made about these principles by the courts. However, it has been argued in this chapter that once the actual decisions are examined we can see that that the judges are open to our claims. This is not surprising: good judges have extensive experience in responding to the agonies of human life, and are all too aware of the connection between human flourishing and secure caring relationships. They are all too aware of the harms that can result from abusive relationships. They are aware too that we want to see virtues in ourselves and those we love. Not surprisingly we want these virtues for those on whose behalf we make decisions.

We hope that we have provided an explicit justification for what the courts, beneath the veneer of a narrow, atomistic construction of 'welfare' and 'best interests' are actually often doing, and an encouragement to courts to construe those provisions in the holistic way demanded by the way that relational human beings actually live. The courts should serve humans, not abstractions.

References

Department for Constitutional Affairs (2007) Mental Capacity Act 2005: Code of Practice. TSO, London

Dunn M, Herring J (2011) Safeguarding children and adults: much of a muchness? Child Family Law Q 23:528

Herring J (1999) The Human Rights Act and the welfare principle in family law—conflicting or complementary? Child Family Law Q 11: 223–243

Herring J (1999b) The welfare principle and the rights of parents. In: Bainham A, Lindley B, Richards M (eds) What is a Parent?. Hart, Oxford

Herring J (2015) Family law, 7th edn. Pearson, Harlow

Herring J, Foster C (2012) Welfare means relationality, virtue and altruism. Legal Studies 32 (3):480–498

Manthorpe J, Rapaport J, Stanley N (2007) Who decides now? Protecting and empowering vulnerable adults. Br J Soc Work 37:557–576

Pattinson S (2011) Medical law and ethics. Sweet and Maxwell, London

Tolley T (2014) Hands-off or hands-on?: deconstructing the 'test-case' of Re G within a culture of children's rights. Mod L Rev 77:110–121

Chapter 5
Putting It into Practice

Abstract This chapter seeks to apply the principles set out in the book by considering their application to some concrete examples. It suggests nine principles which we believe capture the essence of our approach. It then uses them to analyse six different scenarios.

Keywords Altruism · Organ donation · Alzheimer's disease · Bodies · Research

5.1 Introduction

So far it has all been easy. We have outlined some history, some philosophy, some science, our own personal convictions, and a (very) small amount of law. And we have airily said that the law should listen to, and embody, what we have had to say about relationality and altruism.

But there is a lot more work to be done. We have to show:

(a) that our theories produce solutions that are consistent with themselves: we are very aware that some theories have to be squeezed so hard on the way to the legal coal-face that little of their original character or purpose survives; and
(b) that our solutions are better solutions—in the sense of promoting human thriving more effectively—than the alternatives; and
(c) that our solutions are practicable: that they can be implemented within the framework of the existing or a reasonably attainable legal system.

This chapter seeks to do that work by testing our theories against those criteria. We set out problems that seem to us to challenge our contentions most brutally, and then see how the contentions deal with them. We conclude by arguing that the contentions have made their case for becoming the legal orthodoxy.

We derive nine principles from our examination of the facts about humans and of the philosophical and legal material. They are as follows:

1. *Every human is related to every other human.*
2. *Not every human is equally related to every other human.*

C. Foster and J. Herring, *Altruism, Welfare and the Law*,
SpringerBriefs in Law, DOI 10.1007/978-3-319-21605-8_5

Some humans are closer to us than others. That proximity arises in many ways. We are genetically closer to our near relatives than to our more distant relatives, for instance. That genetic proximity has some consequences. It may mean, for instance, that my knowledge of something about me is also knowledge of something about a near relative. If that near relative does not know that thing about herself, it may be that in some circumstances I have a duty to disclose to that relative my knowledge of that shared characteristic (Foster, Herring and Boyd 2014). Few would dispute that paternity and maternity entail some duties, and that uncle-hood and aunt-hood entail duties that are similar in nature but considerably diluted. Those diluted duties may be conditional duties which spring into effect only in special circumstances, such as the death or incapacity of the biological parents.

There are many other types of proximity. To a greater or lesser extent the other types of proximity are types that we intuitively assume. The English law imposes duties in tort to our neighbours, and famously defines neighbours as those whom it is reasonably foreseeable will be affected by our actions and inactions (Donoghue v Stevenson 1932; Caparo Industries plc v Dickman 1990). We generally have a choice, of sorts, as to the identity of the person whom it is reasonably foreseeable will be affected. We can choose whether or not to live near X. We can choose whether or not to drive a car, and thereby assume the responsibility towards other road users. Clinicians can choose whether or not to assume a clinical responsibility to a particular patient. The 'of sorts' is of course very important. A legal duty will often look very much like a creature of mere circumstance, but the set of circumstances that has done the creation will generally itself be a creature of (however distantly) our own volition. It is the same with the criminal law. By living in a nation state we impliedly (via some sort of social contract) agree to abide by its rules. At the root of many of those rules will be some sort of notion of proximity: I can engage in acts in the comfort of my own home that would be criminal offences were they committed in the proximity of other citizens. I can place the tip of my knife anywhere but within the boundaries of the body or the property of another. In any event the application of the rules (bar a few exotic extra-territorial exceptions) is conditional on the contractual proximity assumed by our endorsement of the social contract, and/or the physical proximity associated with our decision to continue living within the national boundaries. Proximity, in short, matters very much to the law.

It also matters very much to our intuitions about ethical behaviour. In 'trolley problem' type thought experiments, respondents are consistently much less willing to save five people tied on a railway line by pushing a fat man off a footbridge into the path of the oncoming train than they are to save the five by pulling a lever and diverting the train onto a branch line on which one is tied. The utilitarian calculus is identical in each case, but our intuitions say very different things. Similarly, we would not hesitate to pay £5 to save the life of a child (any child) in the same room as us, but will not give £5 on our credit card to save the life of a child in Africa.

The differences between our reactions in these types of circumstances have been trenchantly denounced by many philosophers (e.g. Singer 2005; Rand, Greene and Nowak 2012; Greene 2003; Haidt and Joseph 2007). The denunciations are powerful, but they are generally couched (at least in the cases of Peter Singer and

Joshua Greene), as part of an apologia for an unnuanced, reductionist utilitarianism that embodies a sort of evolutionary snobbery. For them, intuitions are crude, primitive heuristics that did reasonable service when we were evolutionarily younger and had less developed cerebral cortices. Intuitions unfortunately linger, and often trump cognition. This, for them, is a triumph of darkness over light; of chaos over order. We can and should do better, they say. Greene compares human psychology to an SLR camera. We can keep our minds on automatic settings (analogous to the fast, intuitive responses), or we can intelligently adjust the settings to the light conditions and the sort of picture we want (analogous to cognition). Generally the automatic settings will do a good enough job, but if you want really excellent pictures of a particular type you will have to take the trouble to use the manual controls. Cognition gives bespoke ethical solutions; intuition gives shabby, often ill-fitting solutions (Greene 2014). This is not the place for a detailed dissection of those claims. It is enough for now to say that our intuitions are vertiginously ancient and deeply embedded. They probably tell us something worth listening to about the way that we should live in order to thrive, but even if they don't, there is simply no way that they can be ignored. Even if they are stupid, they have to be humoured to some degree. This is not to say, of course, that all our intuitions deserve respect. Some are plainly culturally conditioned and plainly wrong. Until recently many in western Europe thought that bear-baiting was a good way to spend an afternoon, and framed their ethical and legal codes accordingly. The underlying intuitions have been rightly revisited and overridden in the minds of all civilized people. But such examples do not justify the dismissal of intuitions. At the very least they need to be listened to and interrogated. They often have something enlightening to say.

3. *The basic principle of utilitarianism is correct*

We observed in Chap. 2 that utilitarianism, at least in its original, Benthamite form, was the purest philosophical expression of altruism and communitarianism. The greatest happiness of the greatest number should always be a primary, if not *the* primary, concern both of governments and of individuals. It follows from principles 1 and 2 above that it is not possible to distinguish neatly between the good of an individual and the good of the community of which she forms a part, and accordingly that some (but not all) difficult questions about what constitutes the good of the individual can be answered by asking 'What will maximize the *eudaimonia* of the community?'

Of course one must be tremendously careful about this. Individual and community interests, although very closely, dynamically related, are not identical. We would prefer to say that to act towards an individual in a way that is not (taking all things in consideration, including her nexus with the community) in her best interests, is not in the wider interests of the community either. Only such an elliptical formulation captures the curious relationship between the individual and society, and exorcises the spectre of the icy, tyrannous consequentialist, who does not hesitate to sacrifice the individual on the basis of some spurious calculus.

4. *Community and altruism are essential elements of human thriving*

This is true however one defines thriving. We have set out some of the evidence for this proposition in Chap. 2.

5. *The only justification for law is the promotion of human thriving*

6. *Ethics and law are not the same*

Law is frightening. It should be a last resort. It should tend to encourage ethical behaviour (this follows from principle 5 above), but a society that seeks to put all its ethics onto the statute book is a nasty one (Foster and Miola 2015).

7. *The determination of an individual's best interests is a holistic exercise, identical with the identification of the factors that will maximize that individual's thriving*

This necessarily requires that one takes into account the community ties of the individual, since those interests are part of the definition of the individual. To identify the interests of the individual solely in terms of her autonomy begs too many questions to be satisfactory. There are, for instance, many different accounts of autonomy: mere 'self-determination' is a formulation too vague to be meaningful. The three main conceptions (Coggon 2007) are ideal desire autonomy (which reflects what a person *should* want, measured by reference to a supposedly universal or objective standard), current desire autonomy (reflecting 'immediate inclinations') (e.g. Glover 1977), and best desire autonomy (which reflects someone's overall desires, seen in the light of their values: this may well, and often does, conflict with their immediate desires.) (e.g. Frankfurt 1988; Dworkin 1988). When the law well-meaningly seeks to maximize the 'autonomy' of a person, it is generally unclear which of these types of autonomy is its object. We wholly acknowledge that it would be a frightening society which did not make some sort of autonomy interests central, if not paramount, in its determination of the 'best interests' of a person. In the light of our survey of what actually makes humans thrive, and on the assumption that each right-thinking person would autonomously decide that they wanted to thrive, we consider that autonomy, in the sense that should be honoured by such statutes as the Children Act 1989 and the Mental Capacity Act 2005, is indeed honoured by an account that sees ideal desire autonomy and best desire autonomy as *ultimately identical*—mandating a decision for the individual that asserts her to be essentially relational and altruistic.

8. *Human bodies matter, but there is no place for vitalism*

Since humans are embodied animals, and our bodies are important instruments in the business of thriving, what happens to human bodies matters. But there is a time for dying: one cannot spell out of any 'thriving' approach to the ascertainment of 'best interests' the notion that biological life should be maintained at all costs.

9. *Resources are limited, and that has ethical corollaries*

Healthcare budgets, at least in a publicly funded healthcare system, are distinctly finite. Disease, degeneration and trauma generate an inexhaustible appetite for the available funds. Hence one man's treatment is another man's denial of treatment. To save or enable one is to kill or disable another. To be consistent, we have to propose that these agonizing dilemmas can and should be resolved by recourse to an audit of 'thriving' interests. One will have to ask, in reference to any proposed decision about resource allocation, how the net amount of human thriving will be affected by that decision. This is easier said than done. In undertaking that curious audit, one will bear in mind that there are many stakeholders to any anticipated transaction, all of whose thriving may be affected to a greater or lesser extent: one should not take into account simply the patients who are scrambling for the available resources: relatives, clinicians and society generally will also have relevant interests (Foster 2014a, b). This is, really, no more than the balancing of individual and societal interests demanded by the constructive tension between Article 8(1) and 8(2) of the ECHR. If one can see all medico-legal questions through the prism of Article 8 (and we think that one can and should), then this, although it sounds eccentric, no more than a statement of the existing legal obligations in resource allocation cases.

With these nine principles in mind, we turn to the problems of real life. We decided to set one another problems that would test our principles. The first three problems were set by JH and answered by CF. The final three were set by CF and answered by JH. To avoid repetition, we indicate in each case, by reference to the number of the principle in the above list, which principles we rely on to support the argument.

5.2 Scenario 1

A very wealthy man, X, has lost capacity. There is an earthquake in an impoverished country and a plea for aid. Should some of the man's money, for which he has no need, be sent as a contribution?

No. It would have been good if he had chosen to send some before he became incapacitous, but his decision not to do so should be regarded, consistently with the Mental Capacity Act 2005, as indicating something at least about his present presumed wishes (Section 4(6)). We note that ethics and law are different (6), and that accordingly, although the law will want to encourage ethical behaviour (and sending money to the charity would certainly be ethical), the law should be very reluctant to trump the wishes which it can be presumed someone would hold if capacitous. Communitarianism and the centrality of altruism to human definition and thriving do not justify theft. In support of our presumption that X would not have chosen to send money himself, we note the evidence that, ethically, to be out of sight is out of mind: see 2.

This may dispose of the question put, but the answer might be different (all these cases will be crucially fact-sensitive), if the proximity between X and the donee were closer: 1 and 2. There we would recruit 3, 4 and 7, and we may well argue that a donation should be made in the best interests not only of the donor but the donee: we would insist that those interests were intimately interrelated, and that the inability of the donor to know that he had conferred a benefit would not mean that the good he had done was incapable of being a genuine benefit to him. Subjective appreciation of a good is not central to its goodness. We note that where a testator has made inadequate provision for family and dependents, the court can 'correct' the provision (Inheritance (Provision for Family and Dependants) Act 1975). That is analogous to the sort of redistribution of wealth that is envisaged in extracting X's money from his account and giving it to, for instance, a local charity in which he had previously taken an interest. When the court makes such a correction, we suggest that it is acknowledging (or at least should acknowledge) the force of principles 1, 2 (insofar as it acknowledges the importance of proximity), 3, 4, 5, 7 and, arguably, 9.

5.3 Scenario 2

> Professor Z is an expert on Alzheimer's Disease. He has developed a new form of brain surgery which he thinks might help in very advanced cases of Alzheimer's Disease. Can patients who lack capacity be used in the surgery?

It depends—particularly on whether it is feasible to undertake comparable research on competent patients, on the likelihood that the experimentation will produce a medically tectonic result, and on whether the cohort of patients used in the experimentation might themselves be beneficiaries of the possible treatment, and whether, if the experimentees themselves might not be helped, others in a comparable class might be potential beneficiaries.

We note that many of these concerns are reflected in the World Medical Association's Declaration of Helsinki (2013), which contains the most authoritative set of guidelines about research on human subjects. It specifies, inter alia, that '[m]edical research involving human subjects may only be conducted if the importance of the objective outweighs the risks and burdens to the research subjects' (para 16) and that '[m]edical research with a vulnerable group is only justified if the research is responsive to the health needs or priorities of this group and the research cannot be carried out in a non-vulnerable group. In addition, this group should stand to benefit from the knowledge, practices or interventions that result from the research.' (para 20)

This second citation from the Declaration is particularly interesting. We suggest that it illustrates that altruism is already recognized by the international community as being in the best interests of a person. Note that, to be justifiable, the experimental technique need not potentially benefit the individual subjects themselves. They are assumed (an illustration of 1 and the proximity elements of 2) to be defined partly by reference to their membership of the community of persons sharing the same medical condition. Even if they do not live to benefit directly from the research, the intervention is justified *since other members of the community may benefit*. A benefit to the community is deemed to be a benefit to each member of it, even if not all members benefit.

English lawyers would hesitate long before saying that this type of benefit to the cohort could be classified as an individual interest sufficient to justify this experimental surgery. They would quote s. 4 of the Mental Capacity Act 2005 as authority for the proposition that any overall medical detriment (such as would be entailed in the brain surgery) would mean that the surgery itself could not be in the patient's best interests. But we do not read s. 4 so narrowly. The section is elastic enough to accommodate our analysis and allow the surgery as in the patient's overall best interests in some circumstances. The easiest routes to this conclusion would be to say that the patient whose best interests fell to be considered could only be identified by reference to the community of which she was a part, and that her own best interests entailed making a contribution to that community.

5.4 Scenario 3

Ms. A is preparing a documentary on the terrible conditions in care homes. She has footage of incapacitous patients being sexually assaulted and allowed to wander naked in the care home. She wishes to broadcast the material. Should she be allowed to do so?

The law is accustomed to dealing with such questions. There are two broad approaches, both of which generally reach the same conclusion. The traditional approach is to ask whether the public interest in disclosure outweighs the public interest in non-disclosure. (W v Egdell (1990); X v Y (1988)). The alternative approach recognizes that (on the facts of this case), the patients have rights under Article 8(1) of the ECHR (which provides that 'Everyone has the right to respect for his private and family life, his home and his correspondence', but that there may be no overall breach of Article 8 if the broadcast was justified under the provisions of the general societal considerations of Article 8(2), which reads: 'There shall be no interference by a public authority with the exercise of this right except such as is in accordance with the law and is necessary in a democratic society in the interests of national security, public safety or the economic well being of the country, for the prevention of disorder or crime, for the protection of health or morals, or for the protection of the rights and freedoms of others.' Article 10 of the ECHR (the right to freedom of expression), also plays a part—generally buttressing the Article 8(2) submissions of the would-be broadcaster.[1]

[1]Article 10 provides that: '1. Everyone has the right to freedom of expression. This right shall include freedom to hold opinions and to receive and impart information and ideas without interference by public authority and regardless of frontiers. This article shall not prevent States from requiring the licensing of broadcasting, television or cinema enterprises. 2. The exercise of these freedoms, since it carries with it duties and responsibilities, may be subject to such formalities, conditions, restrictions or penalties as are prescribed by law and are necessary in a democratic society, in the interests of national security, territorial integrity or public safety, for the prevention of disorder or crime, for the protection of health or morals, for the protection of the

Either of those approaches would be likely to produce a result in this case that would accord with the one reached by our route. What would the result be? It would depend on all the facts that would be canvassed in the discussion between Article 8(1) and Article 8(2), or between the competing public interests in the traditional analysis. Our contribution (drawn from principles 1, 3, 4 and 7), would be to contend that the interests of the patients (the Article 8(1) interests, if you please), *were,* to some extent at least, the same as the wider interests under Article 8(2). That is not just because the patients might stand to benefit themselves from the whistle being blown on nefarious practices, but because, just as in the Helsinki Declaration case, they thrive when others do, even if they are not themselves direct beneficiaries of a change in practice/a new treatment.

5.5 Scenario 4

> Organ donation should be compulsory. It should be assumed that it is in the patient's best interests to know that their organs will be used after their deaths, and even if they don't know it, it is in their best interests to be part of a society that embodies the presumption that altruism is good. Discuss.

I would be perfectly happy to accept that consequence. I will explain why using the approach we are advocating. However, I will then set out how using the same approach one might argue against it. I realise that in doing so I am inviting the reader to say "Ah, I told you: a relational approach can mean whatever you want it to". That, I expect, could be said whatever approach you take. It is possible to use a rights based approach, a deontological approach, a virtue ethics approach, principlism, natural law, etc., to reach different answers to this question. All I can hope to show in this response is that the relational welfare approach asks the right questions.

My argument in favour of the compulsory organ donation would go as follows. As I have argued in a series of articles with P-L Chau, we should understand our bodies as having an important communal aspect (e.g. Herring and Chau 2007, 2013). I will not repeat those arguments in detail here. We argue that although many people feel that their body is instinctively theirs, this is misguided. Bodies are constantly interacting with other bodies. They are changing as cells dying and fall off and new cell are created. We are host to a bewildering array of biological organisms which are creatures in their own right. Our bodies are subject to wide range of forces from inside, the environment and other bodies, which impact our bodies, to good or bad. By the time we die there is little of us that is biologically the same as when we were born. All of these points indicate the falsehood of claiming

(Footnote 1 continued)

reputation or rights of others, for preventing the disclosure of information received in confidence, or for maintaining the authority and impartiality of the judiciary.'

that our bodies are ours, as the product of our labour. They are in fact the produce of communal labour. They are not things we have produced. They are constantly interacting and mixing with other bodies and the wider environment. Nor can bodies be claimed to be owned as property that we control. Our bodies are leaky and unstable.

As Kenneth Gergen (2009, p. 97) in his important book on the nature of the self, writes:

> (T) he idea of the skin as a container seems inappropriate. The metaphor of a sieve might be more relevant, with material moving in both directions. On the one hand we could say that nothing that passes through me is distinctly mine (my body); all that I call 'my body' belongs to the larger world out of which it is but a transient conglomerate.

In a social sense too, as we explained in Chaps. 2 and 3 our bodies are deeply dependent on other bodies and communal provision to exist and operate.

All of these points indicate that the arguments commonly used against compulsory organ donation are based on a misconception. There is nothing remarkably strange about parts of one body moving to another: it happens all the time. Further, we can have no special claim over parts of our bodies because our bodies are a result of and are sustained by the environment, physical and social, all around us. Further, given that our bodies have gained so much from the care of other bodies, the relatively healthy environment we live in, the communal health system, and a very broad range of social provision (from food to exercise facilities) it is little to ask that once we have died and finished with our organs they can be used for others in society who need them (Herring 2014).

I do accept that an argument could be made against the view I have advocated using some of the very principles advocated in this book. While on death an individual's body is, I assume (we don't really know) of no use to the individual, the individual's claim to control is limited,—not least because she is not there to assert it. The body is still regarded by the relatives and friends of the deceased as representing the individual. The Organ Retention Scandal demonstrates that well. The pain of those parents whose children's organs had been taken was undeniable. Mavis Maclean, who sat on the panel hearing the Inquiry at the Bristol Royal Infirmary, reported that the parents felt powerful obligations to deal appropriately with the complete bodies of their children. Maclean (2001) explained:

> The only immediate form of care which a parent can offer their child after death is to arrange the funeral. When this event is based on lack of information about the physical state of the child, this final act of care may for some families seem to be somehow be devalued and damaged.

The body of the deceased, so seen, could still be seen to have relational value for the relatives. The intimate connection they have with the deceased could be said to count against the proposal.

In the end, I am not convinced that that argument counterbalances the broader social claims of the community. The responsibility of the deceased and their community to repay back what their bodies have gained from the social and environmental surroundings trumps the relational claims.

5.6 Scenario 5

> People should be encouraged to have PAS so that their organs can be harvested. They should have PAS when they are still fit, so that their organs are in good condition. Do you agree?

This, of course, raises the same issue but with higher stakes. Am I willing to take my views to the extreme of requiring people to have Physician Assisted Suicide? This is similar to the famous proposal "The Survival Lottery" put forward by Professor John Harris (1975). He, however, infamously advocated that the organs of live people should be used against their wishes to save the lives of others. The simple utilitarian claim was that by killing one we might save many.

An easy way to avoid the question would be to say that if we adopted the proposal in problem 4 there would be no need to have this more dramatic proposal. But that, I realise, would be to duck the issue.

The key for me is to ask what is a reasonable obligation to expect from citizens as part of the "give and take" of communal life. What can we reasonably expect of each other? There are clearly limits to this. So far as the proposal that people should be expected in the prime of their life to have Physician Assisted Suicide to use their organs is concerned, this seems to demand too much. Indeed even John Harris's proposal is generally taken to be a thought experiment, rather than a seriously proposed policy.

More realistically we might ask whether, if a person is close to the end of their life, PAS might be used to shorten their life to enable the use of fresh organs. Wilkinson and Savulescu (2012) have argued in favour of precisely this:

> It would give individuals the greatest chance of being able to help others with their organs after death. It would increase patient autonomy. It would reduce the chance of suffering during the dying process. We argue that patients should be given the choice of whether and how they would like to donate their organs in the event of withdrawal of life support in intensive care. Continuing current transplantation practice comes at the cost of death and prolonged organ failure. We should seriously consider all of the alternatives.

The attraction of this proposal to them lies in autonomy. It would mean that a person could have their wishes to donate met. I would rather argue in terms of meeting our responsibilities to the broader communal good. Where the loss of life is minimal in terms of time, it seems a reasonable demand to make. It is far less burdensome than, say, jury service. However, I accept there may be cases where the loss of a few hours of life would be of enormous value, for example where a person lost the opportunity to say farewell to a loved one. In short, I would support this proposal, assuming it is aimed at those with very little time to live and they do not have especially important matters to deal with.

5.7 Scenario 6

> An NHS Trust gave medication to live patients who were expected to die, in order that their organs might be in good condition for donation when death finally occurred. Assume that there is a law making donation mandatory, but that the organ-preserving medication is painful and confers no therapeutic benefit on the donor. Do you endorse the Trust's actions?

I suppose in asking this question you were predicting that my response that I would accept scenario 4 and reject scenario 5. This proposal is somewhere between the two. The proposal is more justifiable in relation to patients who have agreed to have their organs removed.

As will be clear from the responses to the other two questions this all comes down to what might reasonably be expected of our fellow citizens in the effort to achieve communal goals. The scenario assumed that there is a law making donation mandatory. As explained in the answer to scenario 4 that will be best justified in terms of the obligations we owe following the many benefits our bodies will have received from social and environmental resources. These I think will justify too some pain, especially given the significance of what our bodies have received, and the extent of the benefit to others.

5.8 Conclusion

Have we succeeded in doing what we set out to do in this chapter? We think so.

In none of our answers, so far as we can see, have our principles been warped by forensic deployment. We started off and ended by insisting on the importance of altruism and relationality to human thriving. Where (for instance in the charity donation case) we might seem to have diluted altruism's demands, it is because other principles relevant to relationality (and hence thriving) have had to be accounted for (such as, in that case, the notion that proximity matters).

Are our solutions better? We think they are. They take more about humans into account. We use a genuinely holistic lens, as the English legislation says that we should. In our experience those lenses are in short supply in the law courts. At the very least we say which principles we are deploying, unlike the legal autonomists who typically use 'autonomy' as a slogan, without specifying which one of the several, and very different, meanings of the word they are using. Transparency matters. Our solutions might be wrong, but at least we show our reasoning.

And are our solutions practicable? Plainly, yes. In some instances we come to the same conclusion (but, we say, for more nuanced reasons), as the courts, and in others we concur with the reasoning of authoritative organisations such as the World Medical Association. There is nothing obviously outlandish or heretical about our suggestions.

All we have done, we think, is to try *on the evidence* the case about what constitutes human best interests.

References

Coggon J (2007) Varied and principled understandings of autonomy in english law: justifiable inconsistency or blinkered moralism? Health Care Anal 15(3):235–255

Dworkin G (1988) The theory and practice of autonomy. Camb Univ Press, Cambridge

Foster C, Herring J, Boyd M (2014) Testing the limits of the 'joint account' model of genetic information: a legal thought experiment. J Med Ethics. doi:10.1136/medethics-2014-102142

Foster C (2014a) Dignity and the ownership and use of body parts. Camb Q Healthc Ethics 23:417–430

Foster C (2014b) Dignity and the use of body parts. J Med Ethics 40:44–47

Foster C, Miola J (2015) Who's in charge? Med Law Rev. doi:10.1093/medlaw/fwv004

Frankfurt HG (1988) Freedom of the will and the concept of a person. Humana Press, Clifton NJ

Gergen L (2009) Relational being. Oxford University Press, Oxford

Glover J (1977) Causing death and saving lives. Penguin, London

Greene J (2003) From neural 'is' to moral 'ought': what are the moral implications of neuroscientific moral psychology? Nat Rev Neurosci 4(10):846–850

Greene J (2014) Moral tribes: emotion, reason and the gap between us and them. Atlantic Books Ltd, New York

Haidt J, Joseph C (2007) The moral mind: how five sets of innate intuitions guide the development of many culture-specific virtues, and perhaps even modules. Innate Mind 3:367–392

Harris J (1975) The survival lottery. Philosophy 50:88–104

Herring J (2014) Why we need a statute regime to regulate bodily material. In: Goold I, Greasley K, Herring J, Skene L (eds) Persons, parts and property. Hart, Oxford

Herring J, Chau P-L (2007) My body, your body, our bodies. Med Law Rev 15:34–62

Herring J, Chau P-L (2013) Relational bodies. J Law Med 29:214–227

Maclean M (2001) Letting go. Retention of human material after post mortem. In Bainham A et al (eds) Body Lore and Laws, Hart, Oxford

Rand DG, Greene JD, Nowak MA (2012) Spontaneous giving and calculated greed. Nature 489 (7416):427–430

Singer P (2005) Ethics and intuitions. J Ethics 9(3–4):331–352

Wilkinson D, Savulescu J (2012) Should we allow organ donation euthanasia? Bioethics 26:32–48

Bibliography

Arriaga XB, Capezza NM (2005) Targets of partner violence: the importance of understanding coping trajectories. J Interpers Violence 20:89–106

Chau P-L, Herring J (2014) Interconnected, inhabited and insecure: why bodies should not be property. J Med Ethics 44:39–44

Cases

A LA v JH [2011] EWHC 2420 (COP)
A Local Authority v A and B [2010] EWHC 978 (Fam)
A Local Authority v WMA [2013] EWCOP 2580 (Fam)
Ahsan v Universities Hospital Leicester [2006] EWHC 2624 (QB)
Attorney-General's Reference (No 90 of 2009) [2009] EWCA Crim 2610
Donoghue v Stevenson [1932] AC 562
Caparo Industries plc v Dickman [1990] UKHL 2
Dawson v Wearmouth [1999] 1 FLR 1167
Great Western NHS Trust v AA [2014] EWHC 132 (Fam)
LG v DK [2011] EWHC 2453 (COP)
NHS Trust v DE [2013] EWHC 2562 (Fam)
J v C (An Infant) [1970] AC 668
Re A (Male Sterilisation) [2000] 1 FCR 193; [2000] 1 FLR 549
Re B (A Child) [2009] UKSC 5
Re C (A Child) [2012] EWCA 918
Re G (T) [2010] EWHC 3005 (COP)
Re G (Children) [2012] EWCA Civ 1233
Re JS (A Child) (Contact: Parental Responsibility) [2002] EWCA Civ 1028
Re M (Child's Upbringing) [1996] 2 FLR 441, [1996] 3 FCR 99
Re MM (An Adult) [2007] EWHC 2003 (Fam)
Re P (Contact: Supervision) [1996] 2 FLR 314
Re S (A Child) [2002] EWCA 1759
Re S (Adult Patient: Sterilisation) [2001] Fam 15
Re W (Children) [2012] EWCA 999 (Fam)
Re X, Y and Z [2014] EWHC 87 (COP)
Re Y (Mental Incapacity: Bone Marrow Transplant) [1997] 2 FCR 172
W v Egdell [1990] 1 Ch 359
X v Y [1988] 2 All ER 648

C. Foster and J. Herring, *Altruism, Welfare and the Law*,
SpringerBriefs in Law, DOI 10.1007/978-3-319-21605-8

Legislation

Children Act 1989
Inheritance (Provision for Family and Dependants) Act 1975
Mental Capacity Act 2005

MIX
Papier aus verantwortungsvollen Quellen
Paper from responsible sources
FSC® C105338

FSC
www.fsc.org

If you have any concerns about our products,
you can contact us on
ProductSafety@springernature.com

In case Publisher is established outside the EU,
the EU authorized representative is:
Springer Nature Customer Service Center GmbH
Europaplatz 3, 69115 Heidelberg, Germany

Printed by Libri Plureos GmbH
in Hamburg, Germany